Asian Soup
And Noodles
Cookbook

2 Books In 1: 150 Recipes For Ramen And Traditional Food From Asia

---

Yoko Rice

Maki Blanc

ASIAN SOUPS
COOKBOOK

*Typical Comfort Food from Asia
in 80 Recipes*

Yoko Rice

© **Copyright 2021 by (Yoko Rice) - All rights reserved.**

This document is geared towards providing exact and reliable information in regards to the topic and issue covered. The publication is sold with the idea that the publisher is not required to render accounting, officially permitted, or otherwise, qualified services. If advice is necessary, legal or professional, a practiced individual in the profession should be ordered.

- From a Declaration of Principles which was accepted and approved equally by a Committee of the American Bar Association and a Committee of Publishers and Associations.

It is not legal in any way to reproduce, duplicate, or transmit any part of this document in either electronic means or in printed format. Recording of this publication is strictly prohibited and any storage of this document is not allowed unless with written permission from the publisher. All rights reserved.

The information provided herein is stated to be truthful and consistent, in that any liability, in terms of inattention or otherwise, by any usage or abuse of any policies, processes, or directions contained within is the solitary and utter responsibility of the recipient reader. Under no circumstances will any legal responsibility or blame be held against the publisher for any reparation, damages, or monetary loss due to the information herein, either directly or indirectly.

Respective authors own all copyrights not held by the publisher.

The information herein is offered for informational purposes solely, and is universal as so. The presentation of the information is without contract or any type of guarantee assurance.

The trademarks that are used are without any consent, and the publication of the trademark is without permission or backing by the trademark owner. All trademarks and brands within this book are for clarifying purposes only and are the owned by the owners themselves, not affiliated with this document.

Contents

INTRODUCTION 11

CHAPTER 1: JAPANESE SOUP RECIPES 13

1.1 Hibachi Japanese Clear Soup 13

1.2 Instant Pot Tonjiru 15

1.3 Miso Soup 17

1.4 Kimchi Nabe 18

1.5 Soy Milk Hot Pot 19

1.6 Pressure Cooker Japanese Curry 21

1.7 Chanko Nabe 22

1.8 Mille-Feuille Nabe 24

1.9 Hot Tofu Soup 26

1.10 Japanese Chicken Broth 28

1.11 Japanese Onion Soup 30

1.12 Japanese Ramen Noodle Soup 32

1.13 Bone Broth Udon Soup Recipe 34

1.14 Japanese Squash-and-Soba-Noodle Soup 36

1.15 Torikotsu Ramen Soup 38

CHAPTER 2: THAI SOUP RECIPES 39

2.1 Noodle Broth with Thai Flavors 39

2.2 Thai Chicken Soup 41

2.3 Thai Red Curry Noodle Soup 43

2.4 Hot and Sour Thai Chicken Broth 45

2.5 Spicy Red Curry Thai Soup 47

2.6 Thai Bone Broth 49

2.7 Easy Thai Clear Soup with Chicken and Tofu 51

2.8 Thai Coconut Soup 53

2.9 Thai Chicken and Vegetable Soup 55

2.10 Thai Hot-and-Sour Coconut-Chicken Soup 57

2.11 Thai Lamb Broth 59

2.12 Thai Chicken and Mushroom Broth 61

2.13 Red Curry Lemongrass Soup 62

2.14 Tom Yum Soup 64

2.15 Red Thai Broth with Lemongrass Tofu 66

CHAPTER 3: CHINESE SOUP RECIPES 68

3.1 Quick and Easy Chinese Noodle Soup 68

3.2 Chinese Dumpling Soup 69

3.3 Chinese Chicken Vegetable Soup 70

3.4 Hot and Sour Soup 72

3.5 One-Pot Chinese Chicken Noodle Soup 74

3.6 Scallion-Ginger Broth 75

3.7 Quick and Easy Egg Drop Soup 76

3.8 Chinese Chicken and Sweetcorn Soup 77

3.9 Chinese Duck Noodle Broth 79

3.10 Wonton Soup Recipe 81

3.11 Chinese Beef Noodle Soup 83

3.12 Bok Choy Chicken Soup 85

3.13 Chinese Watercress Soup 87

3.14 Pot Sticker Soup 89

3.15 Chinese Daikon Soup 90

CHAPTER 4: KOREAN SOUP RECIPES 91

4.1 Korean Spicy Beef Soup 91

4.2 Korean Tofu and Vegetable Soup 93

4.3 Kimchi Jjigae 94

4.4 Jjamppong (Korean Seafood Noodle Soup) 95

4.5 Korean Clam Broth 97

4.6 Korean-Style Noodle Soup with Shrimp 98

4.7 Tofu and Kimchi Stew 99

4.8 Spicy Gukbap Korean Beef Soup 100

4.9 Vegan Sundubu Jjigae 102

4.10 Korean Beef Soup with Rice 104

CHAPTER 5: VIETNAMESE SOUP RECIPES 106

5.1 Vietnamese Pho Recipe 106

5.2 Vietnamese Chicken Noodle Soup 108

5.3 Vietnamese-Style Beef & Noodle Broth 110

5.4 Shrimp Pho - Vietnamese Noodle 112

5.5 Vietnamese Pork-and-Noodle Soup 114

5.6 Shrimp Pho with Vegetables.. 116

5.7 Roast Chicken Pho Zucchini Noodle Soup 118

5.8 Vietnamese Chicken Egg Soup 120

5.9 Easy Sesame Chicken and Noodles in Spicy Broth.......... 122

5.10 Vietnamese Chicken and Cilantro Soup 124

CHAPTER 6: VEGETARIAN ASIAN SOUPS............126

6.1 Japanese Vegetable Soup 126

6.2 Japanese Miso Soup with Tofu & Cabbage 128

6.3 Japanese Vegan Shoyu Ramen 130

6.4 Basic Vegan Japanese Dashi-Soup-Stock 132

6.5 Vegan Japanese Ramen with Shiitake Broth 133

6.6 Thai Coconut & Veg Broth Recipe 135

6.7 Thai Vegetable Soup 137

6.8 Veggie Thai Curry Soup 139

6.9 Creamy Thai Carrot Soup with Basil 141

6.10 Vegan Thai Coconut Curry Soup with Zoodles 143

6.11 Chinese Dan Dan Noodle Soup 145

6.12 Chinese Vegetable Noodle Soup.................................... 147

6.13 Chinese Manchow Soup Recipe 148

6.14 Chinese Vegetable Soup with Noodles 150

6.15 Chinese Vegan Tofu Noodle Soup 152

CONCLUSION.. **154**

Introduction

Soup is generally often simple to consume and digest. Based on the kind, Soup is usually simple to eat and help lower, even if you have a sore throat or gastrointestinal issues. Even if you can't consume a complicated soup, your body will usually take stock, whether it's vegetable or meat-based. It's no surprise that your body loves it since it's simple to consume, digest, and has a high nutritional value.

Studies indicate that chicken soup, particularly when loaded with garlic powder, onions, stalks, and carrots, may help avoid the common cold. The heated drink also helps to ease a sore throat. Soups and stews don't take a lot of time in the kitchen. In reality, if you use a rice cooker or a cooking pot like the Air Fryer, you can make a delicious soup in under five minutes and leave the rest to the cooker. If you increase the liquid and vegetable content, you may use less costly components like chicken, fish, and meat. Then, if desired, serve with whole-grain toast and a veggie platter as a meal.

Soup may be a genuinely nutritious meal with numerous nutritional advantages when made with the proper components. Soups prepared with bone, vegetable, or animal broths, for instance, are high in vitamins, nutrients, and minerals like collagen. They also have a lot of taste despite being low in added fats and calories. Soup is also a simple and delicious method to boost your vegetable consumption. Vegetable consumption is linked to a lower risk of gaining weight, a risk factor for chronic illnesses including cardiovascular disease, prediabetes, and cancer.

Vegetables also have a significant concentration of vitamins, minerals, fiber, and plant chemicals, which offer many health advantages. Soups may also be prepared with virtually any ingredient you have in your kitchen. However, some components to avoid, such as thickeners and sauces, may raise your soup's calorie and salt level, turning it into a relatively unhealthy lunch. "Asian Soups Cookbook" is full of soups recipes from China, Thailand, Japan, Korea, and Vietnam. A chapter is dedicated to vegetarian soups for vegetarian soup lovers. Try these recipes and make comfort food at ease.

Chapter 1: Japanese Soup Recipes

1.1 Hibachi Japanese Clear Soup

Cooking Time: 1 hour 5 minutes

Serving Size: 10 cups

Ingredients:

- Ten button mushrooms
- salt
- 2-inch ginger
- 4 whole scallions
- 6 cloves garlic
- 2 large carrots
- 4 cups water
- 1 large sweet onion
- 8 cups chicken broth
- 4 cups beef broth
- 2 teaspoons sesame oil

Method:

1. Over moderate flame, place an 8-quart stockpot.
2. Put the shallot, garlic, carrots, and pepper in the saucepan with the oil.
3. To caramelize the vegetables, sear them on both sides, being careful not to overdo the garlic.
4. Combine the chicken stock, beef broth, and liquid in a large mixing bowl.
5. Bring the water to a boil.

6. Reduce the heat to a rolling simmer and continue to cook for at least 1 hour.
7. Remove the veggies from the broth using a skimmer.
8. Taste, then season with salt as required.

1.2 Instant Pot Tonjiru

Cooking Time: 1 hour

Serving Size: 6

Ingredients:
- Shichimi togarashi
- Yuzu kosho
- 1 gobo
- 2 green onions
- 8 tablespoon miso
- 4.5 oz konnyaku
- 6 cups dashi
- 1 tablespoon neutral-flavored oil
- 1 carrot
- ½ lb. pork belly slices
- 1 onion
- 5 oz daikon radish
- 2 Yukon gold potatoes

Method:
1. Add the onion to the heated oil and coat it well.
2. Then add the chicken and mix everything.
3. Combine all of the veggies and konnyaku in a large mixing bowl.
4. Stir to blend, then finish with the dashi.
5. Dashi should be enough to coat all of the ingredients.

6. While the soup's components are cooking, chop the spring onions and put them aside.
7. Before adding the miso to the soup, mix it in a spoon. Make a point of trying the miso soup.

1.3 Miso Soup

Cooking Time: 20 minutes

Serving Size: 4

Ingredients:

- 1 (8 ounces) silken tofu
- 2 green onions
- 4 cups water
- 3 tablespoons miso paste
- 2 teaspoons dashi granules

Method:

1. Bring dashi grains and water to a boil in a small saucepan.
2. Turn down the heat to medium and add the miso paste, whisking constantly.
3. Toss in the tofu.
4. Remove the layers of spring onions from the green onions and add those to the soup.
5. Before serving, simmer for two or three minutes over low heat.

1.4 Kimchi Nabe

Cooking Time: 1 hour

Serving Size: 4

Ingredients:

- 1 packet tofu
- 100g malony noodles
- 150ml tsuyu
- 2 teaspoon kimchi bases

Method:

1. Break the tofu and veggies into bite-size chunks to prepare the materials for your nabe noodle soup.
2. Combine water, kimchi stock, and tsuyu in a big saucepan and bring to a boil.
3. Once the soup stock has a boil, add the produce and meat first to guarantee that they are fully cooked.
4. Then add the rest of the ingredients and boil in the soup base to absorb the flavors.

1.5 Soy Milk Hot Pot

Cooking Time: 30 minutes

Serving Size: 4

Ingredients:
Broth
- 1 cup daikon radish
- ½ cup white onion
- 3 tablespoons white miso
- 1 cup carrot
- 2 cups soymilk
- 2 3 large shiitake mushrooms
- ½ cup sake
- 1-piece kombu
- 4 cups water

Tofu Ingredients
- 3 green onions sliced
- 3 sheets aburaage

Mushrooms Ingredients
- 1.5 cups bean sprouts
- ¼-pound dried glass noodles
- 1.5 cups napa cabbage
- ½-pound enoki mushrooms

Spinach Ingredients
- 1 cup spinach
- 1 cup mizuna

Method:
1. In a large saucepan, combine all of the components for the soup except the miso.
2. Over moderate flame, bring to a boil.
3. Reduce to low heat and continue to cook for at least ten minutes before serving the mushrooms.
4. While the broth is simmering, you may prepare the other ingredients.
5. After the stock has been simmering for at least ten minutes, carefully stir in the mushroom contents and heat to intermediate.
6. Cook for five minutes once the stock has reached a boil before adding the tofu components.
7. Add the spinach components after the stock has returned to a boil.
8. Serve the soup in bowls with some of the seasonings.

1.6 Pressure Cooker Japanese Curry

Cooking Time: 25 minutes

Serving Size: 4

Ingredients:

- ½ cup apple honey
- 100-gram curry roux block
- 2 medium-size carrots
- 2 cups chicken stock
- 2 tablespoon cooking oil
- 2 stalk celery
- 2 large Yukon potatoes
- 1 ½ lb. chicken thigh
- 1 large onion

Method:

1. On the instant pot, press sauté.
2. Cook for five minutes or until the onion is tender and slightly caramelized.
3. Stir in the chicken chunks until they become opaque.
4. Combine the carrot, potatoes, cabbage, and diced apples in a large mixing bowl.
5. Turn off the sauté function.
6. Press "pressure cooker" and set a timer for ten minutes after covering the lid and turning the steam release lever to shut.
7. To combine everything, stir everything together.

1.7 Chanko Nabe

Cooking Time: 1 hour

Serving Size: 6

Ingredients:
- 1-piece dried kombu
- 1 tablespoon soy sauce
- 2 teaspoons white miso paste
- 4 cups chicken broth
- 2 garlic cloves
- 1 tablespoon ginger
- 8 ounces udon noodles
- 4–6 large eggs
- 8 ounces shiitake mushrooms
- 3 tablespoons vegetable oil
- ¾ teaspoon kosher salt

Chicken Meatballs
- 8 ounces shrimp
- 2 tablespoons scallions
- 1 tablespoon rice wine vinegar
- 8 ounces white fish
- ¾ pound baby bok choy
- 1 medium carrot

Method:
1. Cook udon as per package instructions in a medium saucepan of boiling salted water.
2. In a large saucepan, heat the remaining 2 tablespoons of oil over medium-high heat.
3. Sauté the mushrooms with ¼ teaspoon salt until they are gently browned, and the liquid has evaporated approximately five minutes.
4. Toss in the meatballs and vegetables.
5. Cover and cook for another ten minutes, or until the meatballs are barely cooked through.
6. If using, add the bok choy and vinegar.
7. Cover and simmer for three minutes after placing the fish on top of the stew.
8. Divide the stew amongst the bowls.

1.8 Mille-Feuille Nabe

Cooking Time: 1 hour

Serving Size: 2

Ingredients:
- 50 grams enoki mushrooms
- 3 shiitake mushrooms
- 100 grams perilla leaves
- 200 grams bok choy
- 300 grams beef
- 15 leaves Napa cabbage

Dipping Sauce
- One tablespoon cooking wine
- 1 tablespoon honey
- 1 tablespoon vinegar
- 2 tablespoon soy sauce

Broth
- ½ teaspoon soy sauce
- ½ teaspoon salt
- 3 shiitake mushroom stems
- 6 cups water
- Dashima large piece
- 50 grams Korean radish
- 10 dried anchovies

Method:
1. Each bok-choy leaf should be broken off.
2. Remove a big pot from the cupboard and put the leaves in the bottom of it.
3. Then, on the base of the bok choy leaves, layer each stack.
4. Arrange them in a circular pattern.
5. Place enoki and Porcini mushrooms in the center of the pot to finish it off.
6. Preheat the oven to high and set the timer for ten minutes.
7. Remove the dashima chunks after 10 minutes.
8. Allow the remaining ingredients to simmer for another ten minutes.
9. Remove all of the components after twenty minutes.
10. Soy sauce and salt are added to the soup.
11. Combine the soy sauce, wine, boiling wine, and honey in a mixing bowl.
12. Pour the water into the pot slowly.

1.9 Hot Tofu Soup

Cooking Time: 25 minutes

Serving Size: 2

Ingredients:
- 1 scallion
- 1 egg - optional
- ½ teaspoon saewujeot
- Pinch black pepper
- 1 package sundubu
- 1 cup water
- 3 tablespoons kimchi juice
- 1 teaspoon minced garlic
- 1 tablespoon sesame oil
- 3 ounces pork or beef
- 3 teaspoons pepper flakes
- ⅓ cup kimchi

Method:
1. The pork and kimchi should be cut into tiny, thin strips.
2. Combine the kimchi, pork, red chili pepper flakes, onion, and soy sauce in a small saucepan over medium heat.
3. Stir-fry for approximately 3 minutes or until the chicken is nearly done.
4. Fill the pot halfway with water (or broth) and the cabbage juice.

5. Bring to a simmer, then reduce to low heat for approximately 3 minutes. Remove the scum.
6. Toss in large pieces of soft tofu.
7. Add the salted prawns (or seasoning to taste) and garlic powder and mix well.
8. Cook for a total of 3 - 4 minutes. Just before removing the saucepan from the heat, add the remaining onion.
9. If preferred, while the stew is still hot, break an egg into it to garnish.

1.10 Japanese Chicken Broth

Cooking Time: 35 minutes

Serving Size: 2

Ingredients:
- 1 red chili
- 3 wheat noodle nests
- 1 tablespoon Shaoxing wine
- 150g chestnut mushrooms
- 3 spring onions
- 2 tablespoon rice vinegar
- 30g root ginger
- 2 British chicken thigh fillets
- 3 soy sauce sachets
- 100g mange tout

Method:
1. Bring a pot to a boil.
2. In a big saucepan over high heat, add 1-2 tablespoons vegetable oil.
3. Allow the ginger and chili to sizzle for much less than 1 minute while continuously stirring.
4. Heat for 2-4 minutes, or until the chicken is cooked throughout.
5. Heat for 1 minute, or until the wine has almost evaporated, before adding the Shaoxing wine.
6. Stir in the rice vinegar for 30 seconds.

7. Stir the udon pasta to the 750ml of hot water from step 1.
8. Turn down the heat to a low simmer and stir occasionally.

1.11 Japanese Onion Soup

Cooking Time: 1 hour 5 minutes
Serving Size: 10

Ingredients:
- 10 button mushrooms
- Salt
- 2-inch piece fresh ginger
- 4 whole scallions
- 6 cloves garlic
- 2 large carrots
- 2 teaspoons sesame oil
- 4 cups water
- 1 large sweet onion
- 4 cups beef broth
- 8 cups chicken broth

Method:
1. Over moderate flame, place an 8-quart stockpot.
2. Place the onions, cloves, carrots, and garlic in the saucepan with the oil.
3. Combine the chicken stock, veggie broth, and water in a large mixing bowl.
4. Bring the water to a boil.
5. Reduce the heat to a rolling simmer and continue to cook for at least an hour.
6. Remove the veggies from the broth using a skimmer.

7. Taste, then season with salt as required.
8. To serve, pour hot soup into bowls and top with sliced mushrooms and minced scallions.

1.12 Japanese Ramen Noodle Soup

Cooking Time: 20 minutes

Serving Size: 4

Ingredients:

- 400g cooked pork
- 2 teaspoon sesame oil
- 1 teaspoon white sugar
- 375g ramen noodles
- 700ml chicken stock
- ½ teaspoon Chinese five-spice
- Pinch of chili powder
- 1 teaspoon Worcestershire sauce
- Piece of ginger
- 4 tablespoon soy sauce
- 3 garlic cloves

For the Garnish

- Sliced green spring onions
- Sprinkle of sesame seeds
- 4 boiled eggs
- 1 sheet dried nori
- 4 tablespoon sweetcorn
- 100g baby spinach

Method:
1. In a stockpot or medium skillet, combine 700ml chicken broth, 3 doubled garlic cloves, soy sauce, Balsamic vinegar, a sliced finger slice of ginger, Chinese five flavoring, a pinch of chili powder, and water.
2. Bring to a boil, then lower the temperature and simmer for five minutes.
3. 375g ramen noodles, cooked according to package directions, then drained and put aside.
4. 400g cooked chicken or pork, sliced, fried in ½ teaspoon soy sauce till lightly browned, then put aside.
5. Using four dishes, divide the noodles.

1.13 Bone Broth Udon Soup Recipe

Cooking Time: 25 minutes

Serving Size: 4

Ingredients:

Bone Broth

- 1 jalapeño
- Water
- 3 inches ginger
- 1 head garlic
- 1 bay leaf
- 1 tablespoon black peppercorns
- 1 bulb fennel
- 1 onion
- 6 of beef bones

Soup

- 1 scallion
- Salt & pepper
- 1 teaspoon ginger
- 6 oz. frozen udon noodles

Method:

1. In a stockpot, combine all of your components.
2. Fill the container halfway with water.
3. Bring the water to a boil. Reduce the heat to low-medium heat.

4. Cook on the lowest setting for 24 to 48 hours.
5. When serving, sprinkle with soy sauce to taste!
6. Warm the bone broth.
7. Cook the udon noodles according to the package instructions.

1.14 Japanese Squash-and-Soba-Noodle Soup

Cooking Time: 50 minutes

Serving Size: 2

Ingredients:
- 2 green onions
- Sesame seeds, for garnish
- The seeds pomegranate
- 2 radishes
- 1 teaspoon salt
- The juice lemon
- 1 kabocha squash
- 2 bundles of soba noodles
- 3.5 cups of hot water
- 1 head of garlic
- 1 large onion
- 3-4 tablespoons oil

Method:
1. Heat the oven to 200 degrees Celsius (400 degrees Fahrenheit).
2. Put the kabocha and onions on a baking tray and roast for 15–30 minutes, or until the pumpkin is soft and caramelized.
3. Meantime, heat a tablespoon of oil in a pan over moderate flame.
4. Toss in the chopped onion and cook for a few minutes on low heat.

5. Also, follow the package instructions for boiling the soba noodles.
6. Combine the squash, caramelized onion, steamed cauliflower cloves, salt, lime juice, and two tablespoons of water in a blender. Blend.
7. In bowls, pour the kabocha squash soup.

1.15 Torikotsu Ramen Soup

Cooking Time: 12 hours 30 minutes

Serving Size: 8 cups

Ingredients:
- 4 oz white mushrooms
- 1 onion
- 6 lbs. pork bones

Method:
1. Fill a large slow cooker halfway with cool water and add the pork bones.
2. Over medium flame, bring to a gentle simmer.
3. Place the bones back in the stockpot.
4. Bring a pot of cold water to a roaring boil over the bones.
5. Maintain a gentle simmer for 12 hours after adding the mushroom and onions.
6. Take the stock from the fire after 12 hours and let it cool slightly.
7. Strain the stock after removing the bones using a slotted spoon.

Chapter 2: Thai Soup Recipes

2.1 Noodle Broth with Thai Flavors

Cooking Time: 50 minutes

Serving Size: 1

Ingredients:
- 25g rice noodle
- ¼ lime
- 50g carrot
- 50g green bean
- ½ red chili
- 85g spring cabbage
- 15g fresh ginger
- 1 teaspoon Thai fish sauce
- ½ lemongrass stalk
- 1 lime leaves
- 500ml chicken stock

Method:
1. In a large saucepan, heat the stock to a boil.
2. Cilantro, lime leaf or peel, ginger, shrimp paste, and as much chili as you want are all good additions. Cook for 20 minutes.
3. Cook for another 30 minutes, or until the cabbage is very tender.
4. Simmer for 3 minutes after adding the carrots and beans.
5. If required, top it with extra hot water.

6. Pour the boiling soup over the white rice in a bowl.
7. Serve with a lemon slice to squeeze over the top.

2.2 Thai Chicken Soup

Cooking Time: 50 minutes

Serving Size: 6

Ingredients:

- 2 fresh green Thai chilies
- 1 tablespoon Asian fish sauce
- 2 large lemongrass stalks
- 3 strips lime zest
- 3 shallots
- ½ bunch fresh cilantro
- 4 garlic cloves
- 4 thin slices of fresh ginger
- 8 cups water
- Coarse salt
- 1 whole chicken

Method:

1. In a cooking pouch, bring the chicken, liquid, and 1 ½ teaspoons salt to a boil.
2. In a large mixing bowl, combine the garlic, ginger pieces, scallions, coriander, ½ cup lemongrass, and lime juice.
3. Reduce the temperature. Simmer for thirty minutes, partly covered.
4. Remove the breast from the pan and put it aside.
5. Boil for 30 minutes, partly covered.
6. Allow the chicken to cool slightly before serving.

7. Remove the flesh off the bones and slice it thinly.
8. In a strained soup, combine chilies, garlic matchsticks, and chopped lemongrass.
9. Cook for 10 minutes on low heat.
10. Remove any excess fat.
11. Lemon juice and fish sauce should be added at this point.

2.3 Thai Red Curry Noodle Soup

Cooking Time: 50 minutes

Serving Size: 6

Ingredients:

- ¼ cup basil leaves
- 2 tablespoons lime juice
- 3 green onions
- ½ cup cilantro leaves
- 1 tablespoon fish sauce
- 2 teaspoons brown sugar
- 1 tablespoon olive oil
- 1 can coconut milk
- ½ (8-ounce) rice noodles
- 1 tablespoon ginger
- 6 cups chicken broth
- 1 ½ pounds chicken breast
- 1 onion
- 3 tablespoons red curry paste
- 3 garlic cloves
- 1 red bell pepper
- Kosher salt and black pepper

Method:

1. In a cooking pouch or Dutch oven, heat the olive oil over moderate flame.

2. To taste, season the chicken with salt and black pepper.
3. Toss in the meat to the stockpot.
4. Add the garlic, bell pepper, and onion to the pan.
5. Stir in the red curry sauce and ginger for 1 minute or until aromatic.
6. Combine the chicken stock and coconut milk in a mixing bowl.
7. Add the chicken and mix well.
8. Bring to a boil, then lower to low heat and simmer, stirring periodically, until the liquid has been reduced.
9. 5 minutes after adding the rice noodles, shrimp paste, and brown sugar, toss until the noodles are soft.

2.4 Hot and Sour Thai Chicken Broth

Cooking Time: 25 minutes

Serving Size: 6

Ingredients:

- 1 bunch fresh coriander
- 1 sprig of fresh basil
- 1 tablespoon lime juice
- 1 teaspoon green chili pepper
- 4 ounces mushrooms
- 1 tablespoon fish sauce
- 2 kaffir lime leaves
- 2 chicken breasts
- 3 cups chicken stock
- ½ clove garlic
- 3 stalks lemongrass
- 1 tablespoon tom yum paste

Method:

1. Bring the chicken broth to a boil in a medium bowl.
2. Cook for an additional minute after adding the tom yum sauce and garlic.
3. Combine the lemongrass and kaffir lemon leaves in a mixing bowl.
4. Cook the chicken for 5 minutes in the saucepan.
5. Add the mushrooms and stir to combine.

6. Combine the fish sauce, lemon zest, and green chili pepper in a mixing bowl.
7. Cook until everything is thoroughly combined.

2.5 Spicy Red Curry Thai Soup

Cooking Time: 35 minutes

Serving Size: 4

Ingredients:

- ¼ cup fresh cilantro leaves
- 1 Thai chili pepper
- 3 tablespoon lime juice
- 2 green onions
- 1 teaspoon brown sugar
- 2 tablespoon cornstarch
- 14 oz coconut
- 1 tablespoon fish sauce
- 2 tablespoon Thai red curry paste
- 3 cups chicken broth
- 1 tablespoon fresh ginger
- 1 stalk lemongrass
- 2 tablespoon vegetable oil
- 1 red pepper
- 3 cloves garlic
- 2 large shallots

Method:

1. Heat the oil in a large pan over medium heat; sauté the shallots, bell pepper, cloves, onion, and lemongrass for 5 minutes, or until softened.

2. Cook for 2 - 3 minutes, or until aromatic, after adding the curry paste.
3. Bring to a boil with the chicken stock, coconut drink, shrimp paste, and coconut milk.
4. Add the lime juice and mix well.

2.6 Thai Bone Broth

Cooking Time: 20 minutes

Serving Size: 4

Ingredients:

- 3 kaffir lime leaves
- ½ cup coriander sprigs
- 1 tablespoon brown sugar
- 1 large lime
- 1 ½ cups liquid stock
- 2 tablespoon fish sauce
- 6 green onions
- 400ml can coconut cream
- 2 tablespoon vegetable oil
- 2 garlic cloves
- 3cm piece ginger
- 2 long red chilies

Method:

1. In a large saucepan, heat the oil over moderate flame.
2. Chilies, onion, and ginger should be added now.
3. Cook, constantly stirring, for 30 seconds or until fragrant.
4. Combine the chicken and onions in a bowl.
5. Stir until everything is thoroughly mixed.

6. 2 tablespoons chili powder, lime leaves, coconut milk, stock, shrimp paste, brown sugar.
7. Stir until everything is thoroughly mixed.
8. Bring the water to a boil.
9. Fill serving dishes halfway with broth.

2.7 Easy Thai Clear Soup with Chicken and Tofu

Cooking Time: 30 minutes

Serving Size: 4

Ingredients:

- 1 14-ounce silken tofu
- 1 large chicken breast
- 1 cup fresh parsley
- 1 cup fresh cilantro
- 1 bunch bok choy
- 3 green onion
- 1 tablespoon fish sauce
- 1 ½ teaspoon white pepper
- 5 cups chicken broth
- 1 tablespoon Maggi seasoning
- 3 cloves garlic
- 1 large carrot
- 2 tablespoons canola oil

Method:

1. Heat the oil in a Dutch oven or stew saucepan over medium heat.
2. Sauté the garlic pieces in the saucepan until they are fragrant.
3. Sauté the chopped carrots until they begin to soften.

4. Add the chicken stock and whisk to combine.
5. Combine the Maggi spice, fish sauce, and sea salt in a large mixing bowl.
6. Bring to a boil, then reduce to low heat and cook for 10 minutes, partly covered.
7. Remove the lid and add the scallions, fresh basil, cilantro, and coriander to the pan.
8. Add the tofu and meat just before you're ready to serve.

2.8 Thai Coconut Soup

Cooking Time: 1 hour 5 minutes

Serving Size: 8

Ingredients:
- Salt to taste
- ¼ cup cilantro
- 1-pound medium shrimp
- 2 tablespoons fresh lime juice
- 3 (13.5 ounce) cans coconut milk
- ½ pound shiitake mushrooms
- 3 tablespoons fish sauce
- 1 tablespoon light brown sugar
- 2 teaspoons red curry paste
- 4 cups chicken broth
- 2 tablespoons ginger
- 1 stalk lemongrass
- 1 tablespoon vegetable oil

Method:
1. In a big saucepan over medium heat, add the oil.
2. In the hot oil, cook and whisk the ginger, cardamom, and spice paste for 1 minute.
3. Gently stir the chicken stock over the mixture while constantly stirring.

4. Cook for fifteen minutes after adding the fish sauce and coconut milk.
5. Pour in the coconut milk and mushroom; simmer and stir for 5 minutes, or until the mushrooms are tender.
6. Cook for 5 minutes, or until the shrimp are no longer pink.
7. Season with salt and cilantro, then stir in the lemon zest.

2.9 Thai Chicken and Vegetable Soup

Cooking Time: 45 minutes

Serving Size: 5

Ingredients:

- 2 teaspoons lemon zest
- 2 tablespoons cilantro
- 2 tablespoons lime juice
- 1 ½ teaspoon lime zest
- 1 can (14 ounces) coconut milk
- 2 cups chicken breast
- 1 tablespoon vegetable oil
- ¼ teaspoon cayenne pepper
- 1 (32 ounces) chicken broth
- 1 cup sliced mushrooms
- 2 tablespoons ginger root
- 1 medium red bell pepper
- 1 medium carrot

Method:

1. In a 4-quart pan, heat the oil over moderate flame.
2. Sauté for 5 minutes, or until the carrots, and red pepper are tender-crisp.
3. Cook, stirring periodically, for 1 minute after adding the mushrooms.

4. Cook and stir for thirty seconds after adding the garlic and cayenne pepper.
5. Bring the broth and cocoa powder to a boil in a saucepan.
6. Turn down the heat to a low setting.
7. Cook until the chicken is well heated.
8. Turn off the heat in the pot.
9. Combine the sesame oil, lime zest, and lemon zest in a mixing bowl.

2.10 Thai Hot-and-Sour Coconut-Chicken Soup

Cooking Time: 35 minutes

Serving Size: 6

Ingredients:

- 2 red or green Thai chilies
- ¼ cup Asian fish sauce
- 1 tablespoon Thai red chili paste
- ¼ cup fresh lime juice
- ½-pound shiitake mushrooms
- 1-pound chicken thighs
- Two 14-ounce cans of coconut milk
- 1 tablespoon tamarind concentrate
- 2 fresh kaffirs
- 1 stalk lemongrass
- 3 cups chicken stock
- 1/3 cup cilantro leaves
- 1 tablespoon fresh ginger
- 2 ½ tablespoons sugar

Method:

1. Mix the meat with the curry powder in a medium mixing basin.
2. Bring the stock, sugar, chili paste, vinegar, ginger, lemon, and lime stems to a boil in a large saucepan over fairly high heat.

3. Bring to a simmer after adding the coconut milk.
4. Simmer with the meat and fish sauce, as well as the mushrooms.
5. Remove the fenugreek leaves and set them aside.
6. Combine the lemon zest and chilies in a mixing bowl.
7. To serve, ladle the stew into bowls and top with cilantro.

2.11 Thai Lamb Broth

Cooking Time: 15 minutes

Serving Size: 4

Ingredients:

- 100g cherry tomatoes
- Freshly basil leaves
- 100g mushrooms, sliced
- 50g peas or green beans
- 1 tablespoon Thai fish sauce
- 2 teaspoons caster sugar
- 1 coconut milk
- 1 vegetable stock
- 450g cooked roast lamb
- 3 tablespoons Thai curry paste
- 2 small sweet potatoes
- 2 teaspoons oil

Method:

1. Heat the oil in a big nonstick saucepan and cook the steak with the paste sauce.
2. Add the potatoes or turnips, cocoa powder, stock, and sugar to the root vegetables or parsnips.
3. Gently stir the ingredients together.
4. Bring to a boil, then lower to low heat and simmer for ten minutes, covered.
5. Toss in the peas and onions.

6. Cook for four minutes, adjusting seasoning as needed.
7. To serve, divide the soup among four bowls and top with the peppers.

2.12 Thai Chicken and Mushroom Broth

Cooking Time: 10 minutes

Serving Size: 4

Ingredients:

- Bunch spring onions
- 200g leftover chicken
- Zest and juice 2 limes
- 100g portobello mushrooms
- 1 tablespoon Thai fish sauce
- 2 teaspoon sugar
- 1 tablespoon Thai red curry paste
- 1 lb. Hot chicken stock

Method:

1. In a saucepan, combine the stock, curry powder, shrimp paste, sugar, lime juice, and the majority of the zest.
2. Bring to a boil, then include the mushroom and green onion white.
3. Toss in the meat and most shallot greens to warm through, then serve slathered into bowls with the leftover lime zest sprinkled on top.

2.13 Red Curry Lemongrass Soup

Cooking Time: 1 hour

Serving Size: 6

Ingredients:

- Sea salt
- Cooked jasmine rice
- 1 medium tomato, diced
- 6 cups baby bok choy
- 4 cups shiitake mushrooms
- 1 tablespoon red curry paste
- 1 stalk lemongrass
- 1 tablespoon coconut oil
- 1 medium onion
- 2 tablespoons cane sugar
- Juice and zest of 2 limes
- 5 cups vegetable broth
- 2 tablespoons tamari
- 1 2-inch fresh ginger

Method:

1. Simmer for fifteen minutes with the broth, lemon, garlic, soy, honey, lemon zest, and lime juice in a big saucepan.
2. Return the saucepan to the stovetop over moderate flame and melt the coconut oil.

3. Cook, occasionally stirring, until the onion is transparent and tender, approximately 5 minutes.
4. Add the mushrooms and a sprinkle of salt to taste.
5. Cook, occasionally stirring, for approximately 15 minutes, or until the onions are tender.
6. Stir in the curry sauce until well combined, then add the tomatoes.
7. Simmer for five minutes with the saved broth before adding the and bok choy.
8. Cook for 5 to 7 minutes, or until the bok choy is soft but still bright green.

2.14 Tom Yum Soup

Cooking Time: 35 minutes
Serving Size: 2

Ingredients:

- 300g whole prawns

Soup Add

- 3 tablespoon lime juice
- Coriander
- 1 teaspoon sugar
- 3 tablespoon fish sauce
- 1 Roma tomato
- ½ white onion
- 120g oyster mushrooms

Broth

- 2 Thai or Birdseye chilies
- 3 garlic cloves
- 1.5 cm piece of galangal
- 5 kaffir lime leaves
- 3 cup water
- 2 stalks of lemongrass
- ½ cup chicken stock

Creamy Tom Yum Option

- 1/3 cup evaporated milk
- 1 ½ tablespoon Thai chili sauce

Method:
1. The prawns should be peeled.
2. Place the heads and shells in the pot and set aside the flesh.
3. Bash the garlic, chili, and lemongrass with a meat mallet or similar object until they break open and release flavor.
4. Pour into the pot. Using your hands, crush the kaffir lime leaves.
5. Pour into the pot.
6. Combine the galangal, stock, and water in a mixing bowl.
7. Bring to a boil over high heat, lower to low heat, and cook for 10 minutes, covered.
8. Simmer for 3 minutes after adding the onions and mushrooms.
9. Simmer for 1 minute after adding the tomatoes.
10. Simmer for 2 - 3 minutes, or until prawns are just done.
11. Cook for 1 minute after adding the sugar and fish sauce.
12. Taste after adding the lime juice.

2.15 Red Thai Broth with Lemongrass Tofu

Cooking Time: 30 minutes

Serving Size: 4

Ingredients:
- 2 tablespoon red Thai curry paste
- 300g firm tofu
- 1 vegetable stock cube
- 90g Tender stem broccoli
- 100g brown rice noodles
- 1 red onion
- 1 fresh lemongrass stalk
- 1 lime
- 1 red chili
- 150g courgette
- 4cm fresh ginger
- 1 handful of fresh coriander
- 200ml coconut milk

Method:
1. Heat the oven to 220 degrees Celsius.
2. Bring a pot to a boil. In a jug, melt the stock cube in 150ml hot water.
3. Tofu should be cut into 2cm pieces and seasoned with salt and black pepper.
4. Cook the tofu in a deep fryer with 1 teaspoon oil over moderate flame for 10 minutes, stirring periodically, until brown.

5. When the tofu is brown and taken from the skillet, add 1 teaspoon oil, bell pepper, courgette, garlic, lemongrass, and part of the cilantro to the same pan.
6. Cook for 5 minutes for each side of the jug's liquid.
7. Simmer for 10 mins after adding the chili.
8. In heated bowls, split the broth and veggies, then sprinkle with the pasta.

Chapter 3: Chinese Soup Recipes

3.1 Quick and Easy Chinese Noodle Soup

Cooking Time: 10 minutes

Serving Size: 2

Ingredients:

- 4 oz Chinese noodles
- 4 leaves bok choy
- 1 tablespoon oyster sauce
- 1 tablespoon soy sauce
- 3 green onions
- 4 cups chicken stock

Method:

1. Put the chicken broth in a medium skillet and bring it to a simmer.
2. Combine the spring onions, Bok Choy or Chinese leaves, spice mixes, oyster sauce, and noodles in a large mixing bowl.
3. Reduce the heat to low and cook the noodles according to the package directions.
4. Serve immediately.

3.2 Chinese Dumpling Soup

Cooking Time: 20 minutes

Serving Size: 4

Ingredients:
- Chopped cilantro
- Asian chili paste
- 3 scallions
- 4 cups bag baby spinach
- 2 carrots
- 24 frozen Chinese dumplings
- 1 teaspoon sugar
- Pinch of salt
- 1 tablespoon balsamic vinegar
- 2 teaspoons dark sesame oil
- 8 cups mushroom broth
- 1 tablespoon soy sauce
- ¼ cup Shaoxing rice wine
- 1 2-inch ginger

Method:
1. Combine the broth, garlic, soy, alcohol, vinegar, lime juice, sugar, and salt in a soup pot.
2. Bring to the boil over medium temperature.
3. Change the temperature to a low simmer and cook for 10-fifteen minutes, or until the broth is mildly flavored with ginger.

4. Cook, occasionally stirring, until the carrots are soft and heated through, approximately 5 minutes.
5. Add the dumplings just before serving, simmer for 3 minutes, then mix in the onions and greens and continue cooking, or until the greens wilt.

3.3 Chinese Chicken Vegetable Soup

Cooking Time: 55 minutes

Serving Size: 12

Ingredients:
- 1 cup snow peas
- 1 cup mushrooms
- 1 stalk celery
- 1 small zucchini
- ½ red bell pepper
- 5 green onions
- 1 cup broccoli florets
- 1 cup Napa cabbage
- 1 (8 ounces) water chestnuts
- 1 (10 ounces) bag carrots
- ½ teaspoon sesame oil
- 1 (7 ounces) can baby corn ears
- 1 teaspoon ginger root
- 2 teaspoons soy sauce
- 1 chicken bouillon cube
- 1 clove garlic

- 1 teaspoon vegetable oil
- 1 chicken breast half
- 8 cups water
- 1-pound chicken thighs

Method:

1. In a large Dutch pan or casserole dish, heat the sunflower oil over moderate flame and fry and stir the deboned chicken.
2. After the chicken is done, stir in the broth, poultry bouillon cubes, garlic, onion, sesame oil, and avocado seeds.
3. Bring the stew to a boil, then lower to low heat to keep it warm.
4. Stir in the wheat plants, artichoke hearts, carrot, chopped broccoli, napa cabbage, red onion, bell peppers, onions, zucchini, and green beans, and cook, occasionally stirring, for 1 to 2 minutes.
5. Stir in the mushrooms and cook for another 5 minutes.

3.4 Hot and Sour Soup

Cooking Time: 30 minutes

Serving Size: 4

Ingredients:

- ¼ cup cold water
- 2 eggs whisked
- 1 ¼ cup chicken
- 3 tablespoon corn starch
- 1 small carrot
- 150-gram cabbage
- ¼ cup tomato ketchup
- 2 teaspoon red chili paste
- 1 tablespoon sugar
- ¼ cup vinegar
- ½ teaspoon red chili powder
- 2 tablespoon soy sauce
- 6 cups chicken stock
- ½ teaspoon white pepper
- ½ teaspoon salt

Method:

1. In a medium-sized saucepan over medium heat, add the poultry (or vegetarian) stock.
2. Salt, sea salt, red chili powder, sesame oil, vinegar, ketchup, and chili paste should all be added at this point.

3. Bring this to a boil, then include the carrot, onions, and chicken that has been cooked.
4. Cook for 8–10 minutes, or until the chicken and veggies are well warmed, then create a cornflour slurry by combining the cornstarch in boiling.
5. Cook for 2 minutes, or until the soup thickens, after adding the cornflour slurry.

3.5 One-Pot Chinese Chicken Noodle Soup

Cooking Time: 15 minutes

Serving Size: 4

Ingredients:

- 300g pouch thick noodles
- 4 spring onions
- 20g pickled pink ginger
- ½ Chinese cabbage
- 1l chicken stock
- 80g leftover roast chicken
- 1 tablespoon honey
- 1 red chili
- 3 tablespoon dark soy sauce

Method:

1. Pour the sugar over the bottom of a big pot and let it caramelize for a few minutes, pour in the soy sauce, boil, add half of the chili and the chicken broth, and cook over medium heat.
2. Simmer for another five minutes with the chicken and garlic if using.
3. Cook the broccoli and noodles together.
4. Pour into serving dishes and top with the remaining chili and spring onions.

3.6 Scallion-Ginger Broth

Cooking Time: 15 minutes

Serving Size: 4

Ingredients:

- 1 tablespoon fish sauce
- 1 tablespoon lemon juice
- 1 garlic clove
- 4 cups chicken broth
- 4 scallions
- 1-inch piece ginger
- 1 teaspoon vegetable oil

Method:

1. Heat the oil in a large pan over medium heat.
2. Add the scallion greens, onion, and garlic and simmer, constantly stirring, for 3 minutes, or until the scallions begin to soften.
3. Combine the broth and fish sauce in a large mixing bowl.
4. Bring to a boil, lower to low heat, and cook for 5 minutes until the flavors have mixed. If desired, garnish with scallion leaves and lime juice.

3.7 Quick and Easy Egg Drop Soup

Cooking Time: 20 minutes

Serving Size: 6

Ingredients:
- 3 eggs
- 2 tablespoons cold water
- 3 tablespoons cornstarch
- ⅓ cup cold water
- ¼ teaspoon white sugar
- 2 tablespoons soy sauce
- 1 bunch green onions
- 1 (49.5 ounces) can of chicken broth

Method:
1. In a large saucepan, boil the chicken stock and spring onions over moderate flame.
2. Whisk together the sugar, sesame oil, tapioca, and 1/3 cup cold water in a mixing basin until smooth.
3. Reduce the heat to low and add the soy sauce combination to the soup.
4. Reduce bring to a simmer after 1 minute of boiling on high.
5. 3 eggs and 2 tablespoons cold water, whisked together.
6. Stir the egg mixture into the soup with a fork until the eggs are opaque, approximately 2 minutes.

3.8 Chinese Chicken and Sweetcorn Soup

Cooking Time: 20 minutes

Serving Size: 6

Ingredients:
- 15ml sesame oil
- 2 spring onions
- 2 cooked chicken breasts
- 2 eggs, whisked
- 1.5ℓ chicken stock
- 15ml light soy sauce
- 2 cobs sweetcorn kernels
- 45ml cornflour
- 2 garlic cloves
- 2.5cm ginger
- 15ml vegetable oil

Method:
1. In a medium skillet, fry the onions and ginger for 30 seconds in the oil.
2. Fry for 5 minutes after adding the cabbage and soy sauce.
3. Pour in the liquid and bring to a boil.
4. In a cup, combine the cornflour and a little amount of water to make a slurry.
5. Slowly sprinkle the slurry into the soup, stirring constantly.

6. After a little while, the soup should thicken.
7. Add the chicken and mix well.
8. Finish with a dash of soy sauce and a sprinkling of spring onion after distributing the soup into bowls.

3.9 Chinese Duck Noodle Broth

Cooking Time: 20 minutes

Serving Size: 8

Ingredients:
- 4 pak choi
- Finely sliced spring onion
- Grated zest of 1 orange
- 500g egg noodles
- 5-star anise
- 1 cinnamon stick
- 1 red chili
- 5cm piece fresh ginger
- 2 tablespoon brown sugar
- 6 garlic cloves
- 100ml light soy sauce
- 75ml Chinese cooking wine
- 1½-2 fresh chicken stock
- 1.8kg whole duck

Method:
1. Fill a big saucepan halfway with hot water to cover the ducks.
2. Bring to a boil, then reduce to low heat for 5 minutes.
3. Rinse the pan and put it back on the stovetop with the duck and just enough stock to cover it.

4. Combine the soy sauce, sherry, honey, garlic, chili, ginger, spices, and zest in a large mixing bowl.
5. Cover, bring to a boil, and then reduce to low heat.
6. When the broth has been reduced, strain it through a coffee filter and return it to the pan to taste.
7. Remove the noodles from the pot and place them in heated bowls.
8. Ladle the broth over the pak choi and duck chunks.

3.10 Wonton Soup Recipe

Cooking Time: 35 minutes

Serving Size: 50 wontons

Ingredients:

- 50 wonton wrappers

Broth

- 1½ tablespoon Chinese cooking wine
- ½ teaspoon sesame oil
- 1½ tablespoon light soy sauce
- 2 teaspoon sugar
- 2 garlic cloves
- 1 cm piece of ginger
- 750 ml chicken broth

Wonton Filling

- ½ teaspoon salt
- 1 tablespoon light soy sauce
- Two tablespoon Chinese cooking wine
- 2 tablespoon sesame oil
- 1 tablespoon ginger
- 2 shallots
- 200g peeled prawns
- 200g lean pork mince

Method:
1. In a mixing basin, combine the filling components.
2. Wontons should be placed on a work surface.
3. Fill the wontons with 2 tablespoons of the filling.
4. As you work, place folded wontons in a jar with a cover.
5. In a pan over high heat, combine the ingredients for the broth.
6. If there are any white scallions' leftover from the Wonton filling, add them now.
7. Cover, bring to a low simmer, then heat to high and continue to cook for 5 to 10 minutes to enable the flavors to permeate.
8. Before using, remove the garlic and ginger.

3.11 Chinese Beef Noodle Soup

Cooking Time: 1 hour

Serving Size: 6

Ingredients:

- 2 bundles flour noodle
- 2 cups bok choy
- 1 teaspoon salt
- dried bay leaf
- 2 medium tomatoes
- 1 teaspoon white pepper
- ½ cup rice wine
- ½ cup light soy sauce
- 3 tablespoons spicy bean paste
- ½ cup dark soy sauce
- 1 medium white onion
- 1-piece rock sugar
- 6 cloves garlic
- 2 red chilies
- 6 pods star anise
- ½ cup vegetable oil
- 6 qt water
- 6 scallions
- 8 slices fresh ginger

- 2 lb. beef shank

Method:
1. Add the beef leg, 3 onions, 5 pieces of garlic, and 3 brown sugar pods to a large saucepan with approximately 6 quarts of water.
2. Cook for 5 minutes after bringing to a simmer over high temperature.
3. Turn off the heat from the saucepan, rinse it under cold water, and slice it thickly.
4. The cooking liquid should be discarded.
5. Add the cut meat to the pan.
6. Stir in the dark soy sauce for color before adding the rice wine.
7. For taste, add the light soy sauce, followed by the tomatoes. 8-10 minutes of stir-frying
8. Boil the bok choy in its water.
9. Cook for 3 minutes before removing from the oven.

3.12 Bok Choy Chicken Soup

Cooking Time: 40 minutes

Serving Size: 4

Ingredients:
- Coarse salt
- Lime wedges
- 2 heads baby bok choy
- ¾ teaspoon fish sauce
- 4 cups chicken broth
- 1 small jalapeno chili
- 1-pound chicken-breast halves
- 2 cloves garlic
- 1 1-inch piece ginger
- 2 stalks celery
- 4 scallions
- 2 cups water

Method:
1. In a medium saucepan, mix broth, liquid, onion, scallions, greens, lemon, ginger, and chili; bring to a boil over medium temperature.
2. Reduce the heat to medium-low and add the chicken.
3. Take the chicken out of the soup.
4. Tear into 1-inch pieces and distribute among four bowls once cold enough to handle.

5. In the meanwhile, add the bok choy to the broth.
6. Cook for approximately 5 minutes, or until the vegetables are just soft.
7. Season with salt and pepper after adding the fish sauce.
8. Pour the soup over the chicken and top with scallion greens.

3.13 Chinese Watercress Soup

Cooking Time: 3 hours 40 minutes
Serving Size: 8

Ingredients:

- White pepper to taste
- Soy sauce to serve
- 2 bunches of watercress
- 1¼ teaspoon sea salt
- 5 slices ginger
- 8 cups water
- 1½ pounds pork rib

Method:

1. Fry the ribs gently. Six cups of water were brought to a boil in a big saucepan.
2. Toss in the pork ribs. After 2 minutes, put the water right back to a simmer.
3. Combine the blanch roast pork, crushed ginger pieces, and 8 tablespoons of water in a clean saucepan.
4. Bring the mixture to a boil, then reduce the heat to a low setting.
5. Stir in 1 ¼ teaspoon of pepper after 90 minutes, cover, and continue to cook for another thirty minutes.
6. After 30 minutes, give the soup a brisk stir and filter off any floating particles using a fine-mesh strainer.

7. Sprinkle with salt and white freshly ground black pepper.

3.14 Pot Sticker Soup

Cooking Time: 40 minutes

Serving Size: 8

Ingredients:

- 1 (15 ounces) package stickers
- 1 package stir-fry vegetables
- 1 tablespoon sesame oil
- Salt and pepper to taste
- 2 (32 ounces) cartons chicken broth
- 2 green onions
- 1 onion, chopped
- 2 cloves minced garlic
- 1 tablespoon sesame oil

Method:

1. In a large saucepan, heat 1 tablespoon soy sauce over moderate flame.
2. Stir in the diced ginger and garlic; simmer and stir for approximately 5 minutes, or until the onion has cooked and become translucent.
3. Combine the chicken stock, spring onions, and the leftover sesame oil in a large mixing bowl.
4. Bring to the boil over high heat, seasoning with salt and pepper to taste.
5. Reduce the heat to medium-low and toss in the leftover shrimp dumplings and stir-fried veggies.
6. Cook for approximately 8 minutes, or until the potstickers float.

3.15 Chinese Daikon Soup

Cooking Time: 2 hours 10 minutes

Serving Size: 8

Ingredients:

- Salt
- Fresh cilantro
- 10 ounces 1 large daikon
- 4 dried scallops
- 1-pound pork

Method:

1. To wash the pork, parboil it as indicated in the pictures, then rinse it well.
2. Fill a big saucepan halfway with water and add the meat, radish, and scallop.
3. On the stovetop, bring to a simmer, lower to low heat, cover the pot with a small space for steam to escape, and cook for 2 hours.
4. Add 1 teaspoon of salt, mix it in, and taste it.

Chapter 4: Korean Soup Recipes

4.1 Korean Spicy Beef Soup

Cooking Time: 2 hours 20 minutes

Serving Size: 4

Ingredients:
Beef Broth

- 75g green onions
- 1 teaspoon black peppercorn
- 350 g beef brisket
- 1 onion
- 10 cups water

Seasonings

- ½ teaspoon fine sea salt
- 1/8 teaspoon ground black pepper
- 1 tablespoon fish sauce
- ½ tablespoon minced garlic
- 2 tablespoon soy sauce

Main

- 2 tablespoon Korean chili oil
- 200 g bean sprouts
- 95 g shiitake mushrooms
- 100g hydrated gosari
- 75g green onion
- 3 tablespoon Korean chili powder

- 3 tablespoon sesame oil
- 1 tablespoon cooking oil

Method:
1. Combine the liquid, brisket, onions, fresh basil, and whole black peppercorns in a large saucepan.
2. Cook over high heat, skimming off any top that develops.
3. Preheat a big clean saucepan over low heat, then add the olive oil, soy sauce, bell peppers and whisk to combine.
4. Add the chili powder after the green onions have wilted and stir for thirty seconds, or until the chili powder has absorbed all of the oils.
5. Boil the beef and shiitake mushrooms together in a saucepan over medium heat.
6. Boil for another 10 minutes after adding the bean sprouts.

4.2 Korean Tofu and Vegetable Soup

Cooking Time: 35 minutes

Serving Size: 4

Ingredients:
- 2 large green onions
- 1 hot red pepper
- 1-pound daikon radish
- 1-pound yellow squash
- 1 (16 ounces) package tofu
- 1-pound Napa cabbage
- 3 cups beef stock
- 1 (4 inches) piece dashi kombu
- 5 cloves garlic
- ¼ cup doenjang

Method:
1. Over moderate flame, pour the chicken stock into a slow cooker or a big deep pan.
2. Mix in the doenjang until it is completely dissolved.
3. Bring the water to a boil with the kelp and garlic.
4. Return the tofu, onion, radish, and shredded zucchini to a boil, covered.
5. Cook for 5 minutes on low heat.
6. After that, add the sesame seeds and hot pepper and cook for a few minutes, or until the onions and pepper are aromatic and brilliantly colored.

4.3 Kimchi Jjigae

Cooking Time: 2 hours

Serving Size: 2

Ingredients:
- 2 scallions
- Salt
- ½ cup juice from kimchi
- 6 ounces tofu
- 1 teaspoon minced garlic
- 1 tablespoon cooking oil
- 4 ounces fresh pork belly
- 3 teaspoons gochugaru
- 2 cups packed kimchi

Method:
1. 1 tablespoon oil, heated in a small to a medium saucepan.
2. Cook the kimchi, pork, red pepper, and onion over medium-high heat for approximately five minutes.
3. Combine the kimchi juice and 2 to 2.5 cups of water in a large mixing bowl.
4. Bring to a boil, then reduce to low heat and simmer for another 5 minutes.
5. Toss in the tofu and scallions.
6. Cook for approximately 5 minutes, or until the tofu is heated through.
7. Serve while the sauce is still bubbling.

4.4 Jjamppong (Korean Seafood Noodle Soup)

Cooking Time: 35 minutes

Serving Size: 3

Ingredients:

- 450g Chinese style noodles
- 20g baby spinach
- 6 large prawns
- 6 squid rings
- 6 mussels
- 6 littleneck clams
- 50g summer zucchini
- 120g cabbage
- 35g brown onion
- 2 shiitake mushrooms

Soup Base

- ¼ teaspoon fine sea salt
- Black pepper
- 2 tablespoon soy sauce
- 4 ¾ cups Korean soup stock
- 1 tablespoon rice wine

Chili Oil Seasoning

- 1 teaspoon minced ginger
- 20g green onion
- 3 tablespoon chili flakes

- 1 teaspoon garlic
- 3 tablespoon cooking oil

Method:
1. Heat a wok over low heat until it is hot.
2. Stir continuously for a minute or two after adding the oil, Korean chili flakes, garlic powder, chopped ginger, and spring onions.
3. Add the squash, mushroom, lettuce, and onions to the pan and increase the heat to moderate.
4. Cook until they are gently wilted.
5. Stir in the mussels, small neck clams, prawns, and squid (or young octopus).
6. Combine the rice wine, soy sauce, and Korean soup stock in a large mixing bowl (or water).
7. Cook the pasta while the broth is heating up.
8. In three soup bowls, divide the pasta, shrimp, and soup. Serve right away.

4.5 Korean Clam Broth

Cooking Time: 10 minutes

Serving Size: 4

Ingredients:

- Cooked rice
- Kimchi or pickled cucumber
- 1 green chili
- Toasted sesame oil
- 3 spring onions
- 2 handfuls beansprouts
- 1 tablespoon gochujang chili paste
- 2 large garlic cloves
- 500g clams

Method:

1. Rinse the clams well and arrange them thin in a pot (with a cover).
2. Pour in just enough cold water to cover (approximately 750ml), then whisk in the chili paste, ginger, and green onion whites.
3. Cover and bring to a boil, then reduce to low heat and gently boil for 2-3 minutes, or until all clams have split.
4. Remove the pan from the heat and mix in the beansprouts and chili.
5. Decant into one big or two small bowls, seasoning to taste.

4.6 Korean-Style Noodle Soup with Shrimp

Cooking Time: 10 minutes

Serving Size: 4

Ingredients:
- 4 cup chicken broth
- 8 oz uncooked shrimp
- 1 medium carrot
- 2 baby bok choy
- 2 small shallots
- 4 green onions
- 8 oz dry rice noodles
- 1 tablespoon oil
- 2 tablespoon each soy sauce
- ¼ cup brown sugar
- ¼ cup Korean chili paste

Method:
1. Set aside the last six ingredients after mixing them.
2. Cook the noodles as directed on the box.
3. Drain the water and put it aside.
4. In a big skillet or wok, heat the oil.
5. Cook the shallots, carrot, fresh basil, and bok choy together in a skillet.
6. Combine the chicken broth and the Fiery sauce in a mixing bowl.
7. Bring the water to a boil.
8. In a mixing dish, combine the noodles.

9. Using a spoon, ladle the broth over the noodles.

4.7 Tofu and Kimchi Stew

Cooking Time: 1 hour

Serving Size: 4

Ingredients:

- ½ cup kimchi
- ¼ block firm silken tofu
- 3 tablespoons soy sauce
- 4 cups chicken broth
- 3 tablespoons gochujang
- 4 garlic cloves
- 1 1-inch piece ginger
- 1 tablespoon vegetable oil
- 6 scallions
- 1 small daikon

Method:

1. In a medium skillet, heat the oil on high.
2. Cook often turns until the white, pale-green portions of the scallions, cloves, and ginger are softened and aromatic, approximately 3 minutes.
3. Whisk in the soup, then the gochujang and soy vinegar.
4. Cook, occasionally stirring, until daikon is soft, about 15–20 minutes.
5. Toss in the kimchi and tofu. Boil until the tofu is well heated.

4.8 Spicy Gukbap Korean Beef Soup

Cooking Time: 30 minutes

Serving Size: 2

Ingredients:
Vegetable, Egg, and Rice

- 1 egg lightly beaten
- 230g cooked rice
- 70g bean sprouts
- 30g garlic chives
- 2 stalks shallots
- 50g kimchi

Beef Soup

- Salt to adjust flavor
- Pepper
- 1½ tablespoon soy sauce
- 2 teaspoon sugar
- 700ml water
- 1-piece konbu
- ½ tablespoon sesame oil
- ½ clove garlic
- 200g beef

Marinade

- 1 tablespoon soy sauce
- ½ tablespoon sesame oil
- 1 tablespoon gochujang

- ½ clove garlic

Method:
1. In a mixing bowl, combine all of the Leftover marinades.
2. Massage the meat pieces into the marinade well.
3. In a saucepan, combine sesame oil and garlic and heat until the garlic fragrance emerges.
4. Add the meat that has been marinated.
5. Bring the water, konbu, and salt to a boil.
6. Cook for thirty seconds after adding the kimchi, onions, and black beans to the saucepan.
7. Soy sauce, sugar, salt, and a sprinkle of pepper are added to the pan.
8. Pour the egg over the broth, then add the lemon chives.
9. Ladle the soup over the boiled rice in serving dishes, then sprinkle spring onions on top.

4.9 Vegan Sundubu Jjigae

Cooking Time: 20 minutes

Serving Size: 3

Ingredients:
- ½ teaspoon salt
- 300g sundubu
- 3 cups vegetable broth
- 1 teaspoon garlic
- 150g fresh enoki mushrooms
- 200g sliced shiitake mushrooms
- 3 tablespoon gochujang
- 3 tablespoon soy sauce
- ¾ cup vegan kimchi
- 250g zucchini
- 1 ½ tablespoon sesame oil
- ½ cup scallion
- 1 small onion

Method:
1. Vegetables and mushrooms should be sliced.
2. Make your soft tofu or sundubu.
3. Over moderate flame, heat a moderate pot or a Korea ttukbaegi.
4. Add the sesame oil after the pan is heated.
5. Sauté the onion and onions in a skillet.

6. Cook for 2-4 minutes, or until the vegetables are transparent and heated through.
7. Stir in the zucchini thoroughly.
8. In a large mixing bowl, combine the vegetable broth and water.

4.10 Korean Beef Soup with Rice

Cooking Time: 30 minutes

Serving Size: 2

Ingredients:

Vegetable, Egg, and Rice
- 1 egg lightly beaten
- 230g cooked rice
- 70g bean sprouts
- 30g garlic chives
- 2 stalks shallots
- 50g kimchi

Beef Soup
- Salt to adjust flavor
- Pepper
- 1½ tablespoon soy sauce
- 2 teaspoon sugar
- 700ml water
- 1-piece konbu
- ½ tablespoon sesame oil
- ½ clove garlic
- 200g beef

Marinade
- 1 tablespoon soy sauce
- ½ tablespoon sesame oil

- 1 tablespoon gochujang
- ½ clove garlic

Method:
1. In a mixing bowl, combine all of the Marinade ingredients.
2. Rub the meat pieces into the marinade well.
3. Allow at least 10 to 15 minutes.
4. In a saucepan, combine sesame oil and garlic and heat until the garlic fragrance emerges.
5. Bring the water, konbu, and salt to a boil.
6. Cook for thirty seconds after adding the kimchi, shallots, and black beans to the saucepan.
7. Soy sauce, honey, salt, and a sprinkle of pepper are added to the pan.
8. Pour the eggs over the soup, then add the lemon chives.
9. Turn down the heat and cover the pot with a lid to finish cooking the egg with the soup's heat generated.

Chapter 5: Vietnamese Soup Recipes

5.1 Vietnamese Pho Recipe

Cooking Time: 3 hours 20 minutes

Serving Size: 6

Ingredients:

Aromatics

- 150g ginger
- 2 large onions

Seasoning

- 1 tablespoon salt
- 3 tablespoon fish sauce
- 2 tablespoon white sugar

Beef Bones

- 1kg marrow bones
- 3.5 quarts water
- 1kg meaty beef bones
- 1.5kg beef brisket

Spices

- 3 cloves
- 1.5 tablespoon coriander seeds
- 4 cinnamon quills
- 4 cardamom pods
- 10-star anise

Noodle Soup

- 30g beef tenderloin
- 5 brisket slices
- 1.5 oz dried rice sticks

Method:
1. Heat a heavy-bottomed pan over high heat (without oil) until it begins to smoke.
2. Place the onions and garlic cut piece down in the pan.
3. Add the ribs and brisket, as well as the onion, garlic, and seasonings.
4. Add the onion, ginger, seasonings, honey, and salt, and just cover everything with water.
5. Adjust the salt and sugar as required after adding the fish sauce.

5.2 Vietnamese Chicken Noodle Soup

Cooking Time: 25 minutes

Serving Size: 6

Ingredients:

- 1.5 liters fresh chicken stock
- 3 large chicken breasts
- 1 teaspoon caster sugar
- 1 tablespoon fish sauce
- ¼ teaspoon Chinese five-spice
- ¼ teaspoon black peppercorns
- 1 tablespoon vegetable oil
- 1 cinnamon stick
- 1 teaspoon coriander seeds
- 2.5cm piece ginger
- 3-star anise
- 3 garlic cloves
- 1 lemongrass stalk
- 3 shallots, sliced

Method:

1. In a small deep fryer, heat the oil over moderate flame and sauté the onions and garlic until lightly browned and caramelized.
2. Caramelized onions and cloves, lemongrass, garlic, bay leaf, red pepper, tomato paste, Asian five-spice, peppercorn, salt, shrimp paste, chicken stock, and chicken breasts all go into a big pot.

3. Next, cook the pasta according to the package directions until they are almost done.

5.3 Vietnamese-Style Beef & Noodle Broth

Cooking Time: 30 minutes

Serving Size: 6

Ingredients:
- 1 ½ cups mung bean sprouts
- 4 tablespoons fresh basil
- 4 ounces wide rice noodles
- 2 teaspoons soy sauce
- 4 cups chicken broth
- 1 cup water
- 1-pound beef flank steak
- 4 cups chopped bok choy
- 2 teaspoons canola oil

Method:
1. In a Dutch oven or casserole dish, heat the oil at medium temperature.
2. Cook, often turning, until the meat is just done, approximately 2 minutes.
3. Using tongs, transfer to a platter, leaving the liquids in the saucepan.
4. Cook, constantly stirring, until the bok choy is wilted, approximately 2 minutes.
5. Bring the broth and water to a boil, covered.
6. Add the pasta and sesame oil and cook for 4 minutes, or until the pasta is soft.

7. Return the meat to the saucepan and simmer for another 1 to 2 minutes, or until cooked through.

8. Serve in dishes with black beans and basil on top. Serve immediately.

5.4 Shrimp Pho - Vietnamese Noodle

Cooking Time: 40 minutes

Serving Size: 4

Ingredients:

- 8 cups bok choy stem
- 1 lb. shrimp raw
- 2 tablespoons hoisin sauce
- 1 teaspoon cinnamon
- 2 tablespoons fish sauce
- 2 tablespoons lime juice
- 2 strips lemon
- 2 tablespoons soy sauce
- ½ tablespoon chili garlic paste
- 8 cups chicken broth
- 1 tablespoon sesame oil
- 2 tablespoons ginger root
- 8 oz rice noodles thin
- 2 cloves whole
- ½ teaspoon black peppercorns
- 1 teaspoon coriander

Method:

1. Set aside rice noodles that have been prepared as per package instructions.
2. In a dry medium saucepan, toast cilantro, cloves, and peppercorns for 3-five min, or until fragrant.

3. Warm olive butter in a pan soup medium pot for 30-60 seconds, or until it begins to shimmer.
4. Stir in the ginger and chili garlic paste for thirty seconds to unleash the flavors.
5. Divide the rice noodles into four big bowls and pour the soup into each.
6. Optional garnishes are served on the side.

5.5 Vietnamese Pork-and-Noodle Soup

Cooking Time: 1 hour

Serving Size: 4

Ingredients:

- 1 cucumber
- 1 cup mint
- ¼ pound bean sprouts
- 2 tablespoons lime juice
- 2 cups water
- 1-quart canned chicken broth
- 3 tablespoons Asian fish sauce
- 1 teaspoon salt
- 1 tablespoon fresh ginger
- 2 tomatoes
- ¼ pound linguine
- 1 pork tenderloin
- 6 scallions
- 1 ½ tablespoon cooking oil

Method:

1. Cook the linguine in a big saucepan of simmering, salted water until about done, approximately 12 minutes.
2. Drain the pasta and set it aside. Drain completely after rinsing with cold water.

3. Meanwhile, heat the oil in a big saucepan over medium heat.
4. Cook for 2 minutes, stirring periodically, with the pork, shallots, and ginger.
5. Combine the tomato, shrimp paste, pepper, liquid, and broth in a large mixing bowl. Bring the water to a boil.
6. Reduce the heat to low and cook for approximately 10 minutes, or until the ham is just done.
7. In a large mixing bowl, combine the prepared linguine, black beans, and lemon zest.

5.6 Shrimp Pho with Vegetables

Cooking Time: 1 hour

Serving Size: 4

Ingredients:

- 6 ounces thin rice noodles
- 3 cups cauliflower
- 1 bunch cilantro
- Salt to taste
- 1-pound large shrimp
- 1- inch piece ginger
- 8 oz white mushrooms
- 1 cinnamon stick
- 1-star anise pod
- 1 tablespoon fish sauce
- 1 tablespoon soy sauce
- 1 ½ quart vegetable broth

Method:

1. Bring the broth, shrimp paste, sesame oil, bay leaf, star anise pod, chopped ginger, and prawn shells to a boil in a small saucepan.
2. Remove the green tips of the coriander bunch and chop them.
3. In a saucepan, combine all of the stems.
4. Cook for 15 to 20 minutes, or until extremely aromatic, then extract and remove the solids with a slotted spoon. Maintain a low simmer.

5. Meanwhile, fill a large pan halfway with liquid and bring to a boil shortly before the broth is done.
6. Simmer for 3 - 4 minutes, or until the shiitake and broccoli florets are cooked but still crisp in the broth.
7. Cook for 2 minutes until the shrimp are firm, glossy, and pink.

5.7 Roast Chicken Pho Zucchini Noodle Soup

Cooking Time: 2 hours

Serving Size: 6

Ingredients:

- ¼ teaspoon whole cloves
- Salt, to taste
- 1 cinnamon stick
- ½ teaspoon peppercorns
- 4-star anise
- 2 tablespoons fish sauce
- ½ onion
- 2-inch knob of ginger
- 12 cups (2.75 liters) water
- 2 medium carrots
- 1 cooked roast chicken

For the Zucchini Noodle Soup

- Shredded roast chicken
- Green onions
- 1-pound (455g) zucchini

Method:

1. Remove the flesh from the roast chicken, leave it aside, and put the bones in a large stockpot.
2. Add water, vegetables, onion, garlic, anise seeds, shrimp paste, cinnamon, and peppercorns to the stockpot with the chicken bones.

3. Bring the mixture to a boil, then lower to a low heat setting.
4. Boil for 1.5 hours on a low simmer.
5. To taste, add more salt or fish sauce to the soup.
6. Allow the soup to cool before using. After that, drain the broth.

5.8 Vietnamese Chicken Egg Soup

Cooking Time: 1 hour 10 minutes

Serving Size: 4

Ingredients:
For the Broth

- ¼ cup Chinese rock sugar
- Fish sauce, to taste
- 4-star anise pods
- One whole large organic chicken
- 2 sticks cinnamon
- 1 teaspoon dried clove
- Water
- 1 large piece of ginger
- 1 large white onion
- ¼ cup salt

For the Soup

- Leg and thighs of chicken
- ¼ cup sesame oil
- 1 bunch broccoli rabe stalks
- 1 package fresh egg noodles

Method:
1. Fill a 12-quart pot halfway with chilly salt and water, leaving two to three inches of space at the top for the ingredients.
2. Bring the water to a boil.

3. In a pot of boiling water, add the ginger and onion.
4. In a small bowl, combine the cinnamon, garlic, and brown sugar pods with the water.
5. Fill a large pot halfway with water and add the entire chicken.
6. To taste, add Asian rock sugar and shrimp paste to the soup.
7. Toss the sliced poached chicken into the mixing bowl.
8. In each bowl, drizzle sesame oil.

5.9 Easy Sesame Chicken and Noodles in Spicy Broth

Cooking Time: 45 minutes

Serving Size: 4

Ingredients:

- 2 cups kale
- 8 ounces rice noodles
- 1 cinnamon stick
- 1 Fresno pepper
- 4 garlic cloves
- 1-3-star anise
- 1 yellow onion
- 6 slices fresh ginger
- 1 tablespoon sesame oil
- 6 cups chicken broth
- 3 tablespoons honey
- 1 tablespoon chili sauce
- 1 ½ pounds chicken breasts
- 2 tablespoons soy sauce
- 2 tablespoons fish sauce
- kosher salt and black pepper

Method:

1. Heat the oven to 425 degrees Fahrenheit.

2. Toss the poultry with soy sauce, shrimp paste, honey, chili sauce, and soy sauce on a cookie dish.
3. Meanwhile, mix the onion, pepper, cloves, star anise, cardamom, and Fresno pepper in a large Dutch oven with broth, sesame oil, fish sauce, honey, and the shallots, cloves, garlic, bay leaf, cinnamon, and Fresno peppers.
4. Cook the noodles as directed on the box.
5. On top, add the seeds, herbs, and any other preferred toppings.

5.10 Vietnamese Chicken and Cilantro Soup

Cooking Time: 25 minutes

Serving Size: 2

Ingredients:
- 2 teaspoon lime juice
- 1 sliced chili pepper
- 6 oz chicken breast
- ½ cup fresh cilantro
- 2 tablespoon hoisin sauce
- 2 oz dry vermicelli noodles
- 1-quart water
- 1 cup mushrooms
- ½ tablespoon garlic
- ½ sliced onion
- Three tablespoon chicken bases

Method:
1. Combine water and Broiled Chicken Base in a casserole dish and heat to a boil, stirring constantly.
2. Reduce heat to a low temperature and cook onions, mushrooms, ginger, and coconut milk sauce for about twenty minutes.
3. Prepare the ingredients while the soup is boiling:
4. Soak roughly 2-ounces of dried rice orzo pasta in warm water for 20 minutes to soften.

5. Remove the cooked chicken from the pan and cut it into tiny pieces.
6. Remove the top leaves from the cilantro before using.
7. Bring the soup to a boil before serving, and then turn off the heat.
8. Finish with a squeeze of lime juice.
9. Place the softened heated rice noodles in the middle of a warm bowl and divide the contents into two equal pieces. Pour the soup over the noodles.

Chapter 6: Vegetarian Asian Soups

6.1 Japanese Vegetable Soup

Cooking Time: 30 minutes

Serving Size: 2

Ingredients:

- 1 tablespoon sesame oil
- ½ tablespoon oil
- 500ml boiling water
- 1 stem shallot
- 100g taro
- 125g konnyaku
- ½ pack firm tofu
- 70g daikon
- 50g shimeji mushrooms
- 50g carrot

Dashi Broth

- 2 tablespoon sake
- A pinch of salt
- 2 tablespoon soy sauce
- 800ml dashi stock

Method:

1. Split konnyaku into three equal pieces crosswise.
2. In a saucepan, combine soy sauce and oil and cook over medium temperature.

3. Place all of the veggies in the pan, except for the onions and tofu, and fried rice until all of the veggies are covered in oil.
4. Toss in the tofu, followed by the Dashi Broth components.
5. Bring to a boil, then reduce to low heat and simmer for approximately 5 minutes, or until the veggies are tender.
6. Remove the scum as needed throughout the cooking process.
7. Add the onions to the pan and sauté for about 15 seconds, then remove from the heat.

6.2 Japanese Miso Soup with Tofu & Cabbage

Cooking Time: 20 minutes

Serving Size: 4

Ingredients:
- Low-salt soy sauce
- 100 g silken tofu
- 1 carrot
- 2 tablespoons miso paste
- 1 fresh red chili
- ½ savoy cabbage
- 3cm piece of ginger
- 2 cloves of garlic
- 750ml vegetable stock

Method:
1. Fill a pan halfway with water and bring to a boil.
2. The ginger should be peeled and julienned, the garlic should be peeled and finely sliced, and the chili should be deseeded and chopped.
3. Cover and cook for 5 minutes in the stock.
4. The cabbage should be cored and shredded.
5. Remove and julienne the carrots, then add it to the pan with the cabbage, cover, and cook for another approximately 3 minutes, or until the cauliflower has wilted.
6. Add the sesame oil and a generous splash of miso to taste.

7. Before serving, add the tofu and set it aside for a few moments.

6.3 Japanese Vegan Shoyu Ramen

Cooking Time: 40 minutes

Serving Size: 2

Ingredients:

Broth

- 2 teaspoon sugar
- Salt to taste
- 2-3 tablespoon soy sauce
- 1 teaspoon dark soy sauce
- 4 dried shiitake mushrooms
- 1 tablespoon sake
- 1 tablespoon sesame oil
- 5 cups vegetable broth
- 1-piece kombu
- 1-inch ginger
- 3 cloves garlic minced

"Char Siu" Mushrooms

- ½ tablespoon sake
- 2 servings ramen noodles
- 1 tablespoon soy sauce
- 2 ½ tablespoon brown sugar
- 1 teaspoon sesame oil
- 150g fresh mushrooms

Method:
1. Pour in the sesame oil.
2. Sauté the onion and pepper until fragrant, about 1-2 minutes after the pan is heated.
3. Combine the butternut squash, shitake herb, and kombu in a large mixing bowl.
4. Combine the sake, soy condiments, and sugar in a mixing bowl.
5. Cover the saucepan and let the soup boil for 5-8 minutes over medium-low heat.
6. Heat a medium and small nonstick skillet over medium heat while the soup is boiling.
7. Combine the sesame oil, sake/mirin, and honey in a large mixing bowl.
8. Cook for another 4-5 minutes, or until the mushrooms are soft.
9. Pour the soup on top. Divide the ingredients between the two bowls.
10. Top with sesame seeds, chili oil, and nori strips (if using).

6.4 Basic Vegan Japanese Dashi-Soup-Stock

Cooking Time: 15 minutes

Serving Size: 4

Ingredients:
- 2 tablespoons mirin
- 1 tablespoon sake
- 1 (2 inches) konbu
- 2 ½ tablespoons soy sauce
- 1 ⅔ cups water

Method:
1. Fill a big saucepan halfway with water. Put the konbu in the water.
2. Bring to a simmer; the liquid will begin to absorb the konbu's aroma.
3. Combine the soy sauce, miso, and sake in a mixing bowl.
4. Cook for approximately 5 minutes, tasting occasionally.
5. Remove the konbu and let it aside to cool fully.
6. Fill a bottle with the mixture, seal it, and keep it in the refrigerator. As quickly as feasible, put it to use.

6.5 Vegan Japanese Ramen with Shiitake Broth

Cooking Time: 40 minutes

Serving Size: 4

Ingredients:

- 2 tablespoons miso paste
- Pepper to taste
- 1 sheet Kombu seaweed
- 1/8 cup mirin
- 4 cups water
- ½ cup shiitake mushrooms
- 1 large onion-diced
- 1–2 tablespoon olive oil
- 4 cups veggie stock
- 2 garlic cloves

Ramen

- 8 ounces cubed tofu
- 8 ounces ramen noodles

Method:

1. Sauté the onions in 1 tablespoon oil over moderate flame until soft, approximately 3 minutes.
2. Reduce the heat to moderate, add the crushed cloves of garlic, and sauté the shallots until they are a deep, light golden color.

3. Simmer, covered, for 25-thirty minutes over medium heat.
4. While the soup is simmering, prepare the ramen noodles as per package instructions in a saucepan of hot water. Drain.
5. To keep separate, stir with sesame oil.
6. Prepare the remaining vegetables and garnishes.

6.6 Thai Coconut & Veg Broth Recipe

Cooking Time: 15 minutes

Serving Size: 4

Ingredients:

- 3 spring onions
- Handful coriander
- 6 cherry tomatoes
- Juice 1 lime
- ½ head Chinese leaf
- ½ x 300g bag beansprouts
- 1 ½ tablespoon Thai red curry paste
- 175g medium egg noodles
- 2 carrots
- 1 teaspoon vegetable oil
- 400ml can coconut milk
- 2 teaspoon brown sugar
- 1l vegetable stock

Method:

1. Combine the curry paste and oil in a large pot or wok.
2. Fry for 1 minute or until aromatic. Combine the vegetable broth, coconut cream, and coconut milk in a mixing bowl. Cook for 3 minutes on low heat.
3. Boil for 4-6 minutes until the vermicelli, onions, and Chinese leaf are soft.

4. Toss in the tomatoes and spring onions.
5. Toss in a squeeze of lime and a pinch of salt and pepper, if desired.
6. Serve in dishes with green onions and cilantro on top.

6.7 Thai Vegetable Soup

Cooking Time: 1 hour 30 minutes
Serving Size: 12

Ingredients:

- 1 teaspoon saffron
- ¾ cup plain yogurt
- 2 tablespoons lemongrass
- 1 tablespoon garlic sauce
- 1 cup brown rice
- 2 tablespoons soy sauce
- 1 cup white wine
- 3 tablespoons fish sauce
- 1 (14 ounces) can coconut milk
- 6 cups vegetable broth
- 4 cups broccoli
- 1 red bell pepper
- ¼ cup ginger root
- 1 cup carrots
- 1 sweet onion
- 4 cloves garlic
- 2 cups water
- 3 tablespoons olive oil
- 3 Thai chili peppers

Method:

1. In a saucepan, bring the flour and lentils to a boil.
2. Cover, lower to low heat, and cook for 45 minutes.
3. In a large saucepan over medium heat, heat the olive oil and sauté the onion, garlic, garlic, and vegetables for 5 minutes, or until soft.
4. Asparagus, red pepper, coconut milk, stock, wine, shrimp paste, soy sauce, Thai chili peppers, green onions, garlic sauce, and saffron are all added to the pot.
5. Cook for 25 minutes.
6. Blend or puree the soup in stages in a blender or food processor until smooth and creamy.
7. Return to the saucepan and stir in the cooked rice and yogurt. To serve, garnish with cilantro.

6.8 Veggie Thai Curry Soup

Cooking Time: 30 minutes

Serving Size: 6

Ingredients:

- 1-½ cups shiitake mushrooms
- ½ sweet red pepper
- 1 can whole baby corn
- 1 can bamboo shoots
- 1 tablespoon soy sauce
- 1 cup coconut milk
- 1 carton chicken broth
- 1 package (14 ounces) firm tofu
- 1 tablespoon sesame oil
- 2 tablespoons red curry paste
- 1 package thin rice noodles

Method:

1. Prepare the noodles as directed on the box.
2. Meantime, heat the oil in a 6-quart stockpot over moderate flame.
3. Cook for 30 seconds or until the curry paste is fragrant.
4. Whisk in the coconut milk in a slow, steady stream until well combined.
5. Bring the stock and soy sauce to a boil.
6. Cook, occasionally stirring, until tofu and veggies are crisp-tender, about 3-5 minutes.

7. Drain the noodles and add them to the soup.
8. Serve with lemon wedges and basil on top of each dish.

6.9 Creamy Thai Carrot Soup with Basil

Cooking Time: 30 minutes
Serving Size: 4

Ingredients:
- 1/3 cup peanut butter
- 2 teaspoon chili garlic sauce
- 2 cups veggie stock
- 2 cups water
- 1-pound carrots
- Salt and pepper
- ½ large yellow onion
- 3 cloves garlic
- 1 tablespoon coconut oil

Method:
1. Over moderate flame, heat a big saucepan.
2. Onion and garlic should be diced. One tablespoon of avocado or canola oil should be added to the saucepan.
3. Cook for five min after adding the carrots.
4. Season with a sprinkle of salt and black pepper, then whisk in the vegetable stock and water.
5. Bring to a rolling simmer, then turn down to low heat.
6. Cook, covered, for twenty minutes, or until the vegetables are soft.

7. Blend in a blender until the mixture is smooth and creamy.

6.10 Vegan Thai Coconut Curry Soup with Zoodles

Cooking Time: 25 minutes

Serving Size: 4

Ingredients:

- ¼ cup fresh cilantro
- 1 lime, juiced
- 2 medium zucchinis
- ¼ cup Thai basil leaves
- 2 cups button mushrooms
- 1 red bell pepper
- 2 teaspoons Thai red curry paste
- 1 fresh stalk lemongrass
- 3 cups vegetable broth
- 1-inch fresh ginger root
- 1, 13.5 oz. coconut milk

Method:

1. Bring coconut milk, stock, garlic, Thai red curry coatings, and lemongrass to a boil in a Dutch oven over high temperatures.
2. Combine the red bell pepper, scallops, and zoodles in a large mixing bowl.
3. Reduce the heat to low and cook for another 5-10 minutes, or until the veggies are fork-tender.

4. Remove the lemongrass before serving and top with Thai basil, coriander, and fresh lime juice, if preferred.

6.11 Chinese Dan Dan Noodle Soup

Cooking Time: 15 minutes

Serving Size: 4

Ingredients:

- 400 g dried rice stick noodles

Stock Sauce

- 2 teaspoon chili bean sauce
- 1 ½ teaspoon sesame oil
- 2 tablespoon sesame paste
- 4 tablespoon black vinegar
- 2 teaspoon cornflour
- 3 tablespoon soy sauce

Stock

- 2 teaspoon minced ginger
- 2 teaspoon sugar
- 5 cups water
- 3 large garlic cloves
- 4 cups vegetable stock

Method:

1. In a large saucepan, combine all of the stock components and bring to a boil.
2. Meanwhile, combine the ingredients for the stock sauce in a small dish and chop all of the veggies into bite-size pieces.

3. Mix in the Stock Sauce until it is completely dissolved in the broth.
4. Seasoning may be adjusted as needed.
5. Toss the bok choy stems and black beans into the dishes with the noodles and veggies.

6.12 Chinese Vegetable Noodle Soup

Cooking Time: 20 minutes

Serving Size: 6

Ingredients:
- 1 package firm tofu
- 1 package of fettuccine noodles
- 1 bundle bok choy
- 2 cups white mushrooms
- 4 cloves garlic
- ½ yellow onion
- 1 tablespoon white miso
- 1 teaspoon sriracha
- 2 tablespoon soy sauce
- ¼ teaspoon ground ginger
- 8 cups broth

Method:
1. Bring water, broth, sesame oil, ginger, vinegar, and jalapenos to a boil in a big saucepan.
2. Cook for 5 minutes with the garlic, onions, shiitake, and bok choy in the saucepan.
3. Cook for a further 3 minutes after carefully adding the tofu and pasta to the saucepan.
4. Season to taste and, if necessary, adjust spices.
5. To serve, ladle soups into two bowls with desired toppings.

6.13 Chinese Manchow Soup Recipe

Cooking Time: 35 minutes

Serving Size: 4

Ingredients:

For Fried Noodles

- 1 teaspoon cornflour
- oil (for frying)
- 1 teaspoon oil
- 1 pack Hakka noodles
- 1 teaspoon salt
- 4 cup water

For Soup

- ¼ cup water
- 2 tablespoon coriander
- 1 teaspoon chili sauce
- 1 teaspoon cornflour
- 2 tablespoon oil
- 1-inch ginger
- 2 tablespoon vinegar
- ½ teaspoon pepper powder
- ¾ teaspoon salt
- 2 tablespoon soy sauce
- 2 tablespoon coriander stems
- 4 cup water

- ½ capsicum
- 5 beans
- 2 clove garlic
- ½ carrot
- 3 tablespoon cabbage
- ½ onion
- 2 chilies

Method:
1. 12 carrots, 3 tablespoons cabbage, 12 peppers, five peas, and two tablespoons coriander stems are added to the pot.
2. Stir fry for a minute, being careful not to overcook them.
3. Boil until all of the flavors have melded together.
4. One teaspoon cornstarch to ¼ cup water in a small mixing dish
5. Stir in the cornflour mixture well.
6. Finally, try this vegetable man chow soup dish with rice noodles.

6.14 Chinese Vegetable Soup with Noodles

Cooking Time: 1 hour

Serving Size: 4

Ingredients:
- Grated zest of 1 lemon
- 2 tablespoons lemon juice
- ¾ teaspoon salt
- 1 small head bok choy
- 4 carrots
- ¾-pound Napa cabbage
- ¼-pound vermicelli
- 3½ cups water
- 3 ½ cups chicken broth
- 1 ½ teaspoon Asian sesame oil
- ¼ cup soy sauce
- ¼ teaspoon red-pepper flakes
- 1 tablespoon cooking oil
- 4 cloves garlic
- 2 teaspoons ginger
- 6 scallions

Method:
1. Heat the olive oil in a big saucepan over a medium heat setting.
2. Cook with scallions, onion, and ginger.
3. Simmer the carrots in the stock for five minutes.

4. Cook for another 5 minutes after adding the cabbage and salt.
5. Cook, occasionally stirring, until the bok choy begins to soften, approximately 5 minutes.
6. Add the lemon juice and mix well.
7. Meanwhile, cook the noodles in a large pot of simmering salted water until just done, approximately 9 minutes.
8. Toss the noodles with the soy sauce one more in the saucepan.

6.15 Chinese Vegan Tofu Noodle Soup

Cooking Time: 25 minutes

Serving Size: 5

Ingredients:
- 1 tablespoon soy sauce
- ¼ teaspoon black pepper
- 300 grams firm tofu

Other Ingredients
- Ground black pepper
- 1 tablespoon vegetable oil
- 0.5 tablespoon vinegar
- 8 cups vegetable stock
- 2.5 tablespoons soy sauce
- 1 teaspoon sriracha
- 1 stalk of green onion
- 1 head of bok choy
- 4 garlic cloves
- 1-inch piece of ginger
- 150 grams noodles

Method:
1. To remove excess water from the tofu blocks, wrap it in a clean baking paper and gently press it.
2. Remove the cloth and cut the blocks into squares that are easy to eat.

3. In a large mixing bowl, place the tofu chunks.
4. Add the miso and pepper to taste. Put on a baking sheet-lined baking pan.
5. Add the white of the spring onion and the stem of the bok choy.
6. For approximately a minute, sauté.
7. Pour in the stock. Toss in the soy sauce and spicy sauce.
8. Allow the soup to boil after mixing everything.
9. Toss in the noodles, bok choy stems, and freshly ground black pepper.
10. Cook, constantly stirring, until the noodle is done.
11. Toss in the roasted tofu and vinegar.
12. Turn off the gas after another minute of mixing and cooking.

Conclusion

Soup may be a genuinely nutritious meal with numerous nutritional advantages when made with the proper components. Soups prepared with bone, vegetable, or animal broths, for instance, are high in vitamins, nutrients, and minerals like collagen. They also have a lot of taste despite being low in added fats and calories. Soup is also a simple and delicious method to boost your vegetable consumption. Vegetable consumption is linked to a lower risk of gaining weight, a risk factor for chronic illnesses including cardiovascular disease, prediabetes, and cancer. Soup is simple to prepare a meal that may help you get many nutrients into your diet. It all boils down to the components when it comes to picking the finest one. Soup may offer a variety of health advantages when prepared with nutrient-dense components like veggies and lean meats. Cream-based, canned, and quick soups, on the other hand, have a greater calorie and salt content and should be avoided. Try Asian soups and prepare your meals with comfort soups.

RAMEN
COOKBOOK

70 Recipes for Preparing at Home Traditional Japanese Noodle Soup.

By

Maki Blanc

© **Copyright 2021 by Maki Blanc - All rights reserved.**

This document is geared towards providing exact and reliable information in regard to the topic and issue covered. The publication is sold with the idea that the publisher is not required to render accounting, officially permitted, or otherwise, qualified services. If advice is necessary, legal or professional, a practiced individual in the profession should be ordered.

From a Declaration of Principles which was accepted and approved equally by a Committee of the American Bar Association and a Committee of Publishers and Associations.

In no way is it legal to reproduce, duplicate, or transmit any part of this document in either electronic means or in printed format. Recording of this publication is strictly prohibited and any storage of this document is not allowed unless with written permission from the publisher. All rights reserved.

The information provided herein is stated to be truthful and consistent, in that any liability, in terms of inattention or otherwise, by any usage or abuse of any policies, processes, or directions contained within is the solitary and utter responsibility of the recipient reader. Under no circumstances will any legal responsibility or blame be held against the publisher for any reparation, damages, or monetary loss due to the information herein, either directly or indirectly.

Respective authors own all copyrights not held by the publisher.

The information herein is offered for informational purposes solely and is universal as so. The presentation of the information is without contract or any type of guarantee assurance.

The trademarks that are used are without any consent, and the publication of the trademark is without permission or backing by the trademark owner. All trademarks and brands within this book are for clarifying purposes only and are owned by the owners themselves, not affiliated with this document.

Contents

INTRODUCTION 163

CHAPTER 1: INTRODUCTION TO JAPANESE NOODLE SOUPS 165

1.1 History and Origin of Ramen 165

1.2 Ramen According to the Nutrition and Dietetics 167

1.3 Various Ingredients Used in Ramen 168

CHAPTER 2: THE WORLD OF RAMEN BREAKFAST RECIPES 171

2.1 Japanese Ramen Scrambled Eggs Recipe 172

2.2 Japanese Bacon and Egg Ramen Recipe 173

2.3 Japanese Ramen Omelet Recipe 175

2.4 Japanese Ramen with Soft Boiled Eggs Recipe 176

2.5 Japanese Miso Ramen with Boiled Eggs Recipe 178

2.6 Japanese Bacon, Egg and Cheese Breakfast Ramen Recipe 180

2.7 Japanese Ramen with Tofu and Eggs Recipe 181

2.8 Japanese Chicken Ramen with Bok Choy and Soy Eggs Recipe 183

2.9 Japanese Egg Tonkotsu Ramen Recipe 184

2.10 Japanese Scallops and Egg Ramen Recipe 185

CHAPTER 3: THE WORLD OF RAMEN LUNCH RECIPES 188

3.1 Japanese Ramen Noodle Soup Recipe 188

3.2 Japanese Duck Ramen Recipes 190

3.3 Japanese Sapporo Ramen Recipe 191

3.4 Japanese Miso Ramen Recipe 193

3.5 Japanese Shoyu Ramen Recipe 194

3.6 Japanese Tantanmen Ramen Recipe 196

3.7 Japanese Spicy Pork Ramen Recipe 197

3.8 Japanese Roast Pork Ramen Recipe 199

3.9 Japanese Chargrilled Chicken Ramen Recipe 200

3.10 Japanese Lemongrass, Chicken and Ginger Ramen Recipe 202

3.11 Japanese Spicy Beef Ramen Recipe 203

3.12 Japanese Prawn Ramen Recipe 205

3.13 Japanese Ramen Noodle Salad Recipe 207

3.14 Japanese Mongolian Beef Ramen Recipe 208

3.15 Japanese Meatball Ramen Recipe 210

3.16 Japanese Ramen Noodle Skillet with Steak Recipe 212

3.17 Japanese Cheese Ramen Recipe 213

3.18 Japanese Ramen Burger Recipe 215

3.19 Japanese Garlic and Shrimp Ramen Recipe 217

3.20 Japanese Beef and Ramen Stir-Fry Recipe 219

CHAPTER 4: THE WORLD OF RAMEN DINNER RECIPES 221

4.1 Japanese Parmesan and Garlic Ramen Recipe 221

4.2 Japanese Ginger and Beef Stir-Fry Ramen Recipe...............223

4.3 Japanese Peanut and Chicken Ramen Recipe 224

4.4 Japanese Roasted Chicken Ramen Recipe 226

4.5 Japanese Sirarcha and Shrimp Ramen Recipe 228

4.6 Japanese Bacon Ramen Soup Recipe 230

4.7 Japanese Sweet and Sour Pork Ramen Recipe......................232

4.8 Japanese Cheesy Tuna Ramen Recipe 233

4.9 Japanese Ramen and Tomato Soup Recipe............................236

4.10 Japanese Chili Ramen Recipe 237

4.11 Japanese Chicken and Mushroom Ramen Recipe 239

4.12 Japanese Parmesan Chicken Ramen Recipe 240

4.13 Japanese Chicken Lo Mein Ramen Recipe..........................242

4.14 Japanese Shrimp Ramen Recipe 244

4.15 Japanese Green Pepper and Chicken Ramen Recipe........245

4.16 Japanese Creamy Tonkotsu Ramen Recipe 248

4.17 Japanese Miso and Crispy Pork Ramen Recipe 249

4.18 Japanese Shio and Pork Ramen Recipe 251

4.19 Japanese Ramen Noodle Coleslaw Recipe 253

4.20 Japanese Instant Ramen Noodle Recipe..............................254

CHAPTER 5: THE WORLD OF VEGETARIAN RAMEN RECIPES 256

5.1 Japanese Spicy Vegetarian Ramen Recipe 256

5.2 Japanese Shiitake Mushroom Ramen Recipe 257

5.3 Japanese Miso Vegetarian Ramen Noodle Soup Recipe 259

5.4 Japanese Teriyaki Tofu Ramen Recipe 261

5.5 Japanese Tonkotsu Vegetarian Ramen Recipe.....................262

5.6 Japanese Pantry Vegetarian Ramen Recipe 264

5.7 Japanese Marinated Tofu and Vegetable Ramen Recipe....265

5.8 Japanese Creamy Vegan Ramen Recipe 267

5.9 Japanese Creamy Sesame Ramen Broth Recipe 268

5.10 Japanese Spicy Broccoli Ramen Recipe.................................270

5.11 Japanese Cauliflower Ramen Recipe......................................272

5.12 Japanese Hot and Sour Dashi Ramen Recipe......................273

5.13 Japanese Spicy Carrot Ramen Recipe 274

5.14 Japanese Vegan Shōyu Ramen with Potatoes Recipe.......276

5.15 Japanese Ginger Ramen Recipe..278

5.16 Japanese Vegan Ramen Taco Recipe 279

5.17 Japanese Vegetarian Spicy Peanut Tempeh Ramen Recipe 280

5.18 Japanese Spicy Soy Milk Ramen Recipe..............................281

5.19 Japanese Vegetarian Ginger and Scallion Ramen Recipe 283

5.20 Japanese Crispy Sesame Tofu Ramen Recipe 284

CONCLUSION 286

Introduction

Ramen are the most famous noodle dishes in Japan. These boiled noodles are essentially served in various flavorful soups with numerous toppings. Chukamen noodles which are for the most part made with wheat flour and kansui are used for ramen dishes. There are numerous types of ramen flavors in Japan. They are used in different flavors of soups, garnishes, broth, noodle texture in ramens, and this is only the tip of an iceberg. Making a tasty ramen is not very simple if you are preparing it from scratch.

The flavor of ramen predominantly relies upon the soup. Ramen cooks generally train themselves for quite a while to be able to make great ramen soup. Each ramen shop has its own particular manner to make ramen soup. So, there are countless ways to make ramen soup. Chicken bone, pork bone, dried sardines, as well as kombu are utilized to make soup stock for ramen.

You can prepare Japanese ramen soup at home by learning the list of various ingredients that you will need to start cooking. By reading this wonderful book, you will get the detailed knowledge regarding the nutritional value and history of ramen. This book contains over 70 different breakfast, lunch, dinner, and vegetarian ramen recipes. You can easily start cooking at home with the detailed instructions present below each recipe. So start reading and start cooking today!

Chapter 1: Introduction to Japanese Noodle Soups

Ramen is a noodle soup dish that was initially imported from China and has become perhaps the most mainstream dishes in Japan for the past many years. Ramen are cheap and broadly accessible. These two factors additionally make them an ideal choice for tourists. Ramen cafés can be found in each corner of the country. These cafes produce incalculable varieties of this basic noodle dish.

Typical Ramen noodles are long and flexible. However, innumerable assortments of ramen exist that vary from slender to thick and wavy. Some ramen cafes permit you to modify your noodle soup in many ways, for example, by permitting you to choose its thickness (slight, ordinary or thick) or doneness (normal or firm).

1.1 History and Origin of Ramen

The ramen noodle has extended its compass across numerous lands and nations framing profound roots in many of these societies. Actually, the noodle has effectively managed to form connections with Japan's lifestyle and history as well. Ramen has a long history in Japan, changing as the conditions of the nation changed too.

The origin of the first ramen is obscure. Yet, a legend says that ramen came from a dish acquired from China. The principal legend sets up Shu Shunsui, a researcher from China, as the person who brought the ramen formula to Japan.

Shu Shunsui was a Chinese exile of the Ming government who came to fill in as a consultant to the Japanese primitive master Tokugawa Mitsukuni. Verifiable records show that Shu Shunsui advised Mitsukini on what to add to his udon soup to make it taste better. This dish is supposed to be the first ramen that was eaten in Japan. While the facts confirm that Chinese culture vigorously affected Japanese culture at that time. Yet, an authentic record of Mitsukini cooking ramen does not exist.

Another legend interfaces the origin of ramen. It happened when Japan opened its ports to the rest of the world. Japan's ports pulled in Chinese voyagers, and a Chinese noodle soup called laa-mein was brought into Japan. This dish fills in as a possible archetype to the ramen today even though laa-mein did not have any garnishes and was not like the advanced ramen.

The last and most conceivable hypothesis relates the source of the ramen to a shop called Rai Ken in Tokyo during the 1900s. Rai Ken utilized Chinese laborers and served a noodle dish called Shina Soba. Shina Soba had added fixings that looked like todays ramen. These fixings include cooked pork, Japanese fish cake, and nori sheets into one dish. Japan was getting industrialized and more urbanized during this timeframe. Japan's industrialization and urbanization helped in promoting ramen. Shina soba was a modest and filling dish, giving a lot of calories to Japanese metropolitan laborers.

Today ramen has become an image and chronicled figure of Japanese culture and history. Ramen has broadened its span universally all throughout the planet.

Conventional ramen is extremely necessary in Japanese culture. In any case, it is still difficult to get credible Japanese ramen except if one is close to the huge assorted urban communities. Now, ramen can be found at practically any general store. Despite the fact that ramen has now become a worldwide pattern, its profound roots will consistently be appended to Japan's set of experiences.

1.2 Ramen According to the Nutrition and Dietetics

The conventional Japanese eating routine is full of healthy food sources. It has all the basic macronutrients that are essential for a healthy and nutritious diet. Japanese traditional cuisine depends on conventional Japanese cooking, otherwise called "washoku." This cooking comprises of adding fresh and healthy ingredients into the dishes to make sure the health of the individuals is not compromised. This eating design is rich in supplements and may give various medical advantages. These advantages may include improved weight reduction, digestion and absorption, long life span, and overall health.

Ramen noodles are the healthiest when joined with different fixings to make a nutritious feast. Ramen is incredible to use as a base for a variety of healthy dishes and it is not difficult to prepare on your own. Ramen noodles are healthy as they contain protein and carbohydrates in good amounts. Fats are present in a very low quantity that is almost negligible.

You can also add vegetables in your bowl of ramen. This will add to a generous flavor and add supplements to the supper. Carrots, spinach, broccoli, zucchini, cauliflower and peppers will not just give you extraordinary taste, they will give you a decent serving of vitamins, minerals and fiber in each bite. Try adding various blends of vegetables with various ramen flavors to discover the combination that you like the best. Ramen bowls consistently go extraordinary with fresh chicken, beef meat, fish or pork for the protein your body needs.

Investigate the possibilities and look at how easy it is to change a generally extraordinary tasting and healthy bowl of ramen noodles into an even healthier feast in minutes by adding different ingredients into it.

1.3 Various Ingredients Used in Ramen

Following are the different ingredients that are used in making ramen noodles at home:

1. Stocks

Stocks are generally from pork or chicken bones or a combination of the two. Dashi stock is made utilizing bonito chips which is a dried fish. Rather than making your own stock, you can purchase instant dashi stock sachets.

2. Mirin

Mirin is a Japanese sweet rice wine, which is currently broadly accessible in the global food walkways of most of the stores. It has a sweet surface and adds pleasant flavor to a dish.

3. Sake

Japanese sake is utilized in numerous Japanese dishes. However, you can use a substitute Chinese Shaoxing rice wine, which is more broadly accessible. Shaoxing rice wine adds another layer when utilizing delicate flavors in Japanese and Chinese cooking and is fabulous for adding flavor to meat when cooking and in marinades.

4. Nori sheets

Nori sheets are very healthy and usually used in different ramen dishes. They add protein into the ramen. They have an incredible flavor and are loved by many people around the world.

5. Kimchi

This is a Korean derived dish. It is fermented cabbage that is used in ramen noodles as a side dish. Kimchi adds a salty and tangy flavor into the ramen noodles.

6. Japanese curry sauce

These curry sauce packets contain a bar of curry concentrate, which can be broken off in pieces and added to stock bases for a curried broth. The flavor is similar to a Chinese curry paste and makes a great delicately flavored curry broth. It is commonly used in ramen noodles.

7. Soy sauce

It is the most common sauce all around the world. It is added to ramen noodles and imparts a unique taste to the noodles. Soy sauce comes in two varieties i.e. light soy sauce and dark soy sauce.

Chapter 2: The World of Ramen Breakfast Recipes

Having Ramen for breakfast is customary in two districts of Japan, and many nearby ramen shops carry on this tradition. These districts are Fukushima and Kitakata. All the breakfast dishes mentioned below are healthy and are traditionally eaten in these districts of Japan:

Basic Instructions to Cook Ramen:

- Take a large saucepan.
- Add water into the saucepan.
- Boil the water.
- Add the ramen noodles when the water reaches the boiling temperature.
- Cook the ramen for seven minutes approximately.
- Make sure not to overcook the ramen noodles.
- Drain the noodles and add a teaspoon of oil into the ramen.
- The oil will prevent the ramen from sticking.
- You can use this method of boiling the ramen in all of the recipes below.

2.1 Japanese Ramen Scrambled Eggs Recipe

Preparation Time: 30 minutes
Cooking Time: 10 minutes
Serving: 4

Ingredients:

- Chopped chives, one teaspoon
- Butter, two tablespoon
- Cooked chickpeas, half cup
- Tofu cubes, half pound
- Salt, to taste
- Black pepper, to taste
- Tamari paste, two teaspoon
- Eggs, four
- Mirin paste, one tablespoon
- Chopped garlic, one teaspoon
- Ramen noodles, four packs

Instructions:
1. Take a large pan.
2. Add the butter and let it meltdown.
3. Add in the eggs.
4. Add in the tamari paste.

5. Mix the tamari paste and eggs.
6. Add the chopped garlic.
7. Scramble the mixture.
8. Add in the salt and pepper.
9. Add in the chickpeas and rest of the ingredients in the end.
10. Boil the ramen noodles according to the instructions on the pack.
11. Drain the noodles and add them into the pan.
12. Mix all the ingredients well and then dish them out.
13. Garnish the fresh chopped chives on top.
14. Your dish is ready to be served.

2.2 Japanese Bacon and Egg Ramen Recipe

Preparation Time: 30 minutes
Cooking Time: 10 minutes
Serving: 4

Ingredients:

- Chopped chives, one teaspoon
- Butter, two tablespoon
- Chopped bacon, half pound
- Salt, to taste

- Black pepper, to taste
- Tamari paste, two teaspoon
- Eggs, four
- Mirin paste, one tablespoon
- Chopped garlic, one teaspoon
- Ramen noodles, four packs

Instructions:
1. Take a large pan.
2. Add the butter and let it meltdown.
3. Add in the chopped bacons.
4. Add in the tamari paste.
5. Mix all the ingredients well.
6. Add the chopped garlic.
7. Add in the rest of the ingredients in the end.
8. Scramble the mixture.
9. Add in the salt and pepper.
10. Boil the ramen noodles according to the instructions on the pack.
11. Drain the noodles and add them into the pan.
12. Mix all the ingredients well and then dish them out.
13. Garnish the fresh chopped chives on top.
14. Your dish is ready to be served.

2.3 Japanese Ramen Omelet Recipe

Preparation Time: 30 minutes
Cooking Time: 10 minutes
Serving: 4

Ingredients:

- Onions, half cup
- Rice wine, one tablespoon
- Eggs, four
- Black pepper, to taste
- Salt, to taste
- Starch, a quarter teaspoon
- Ramen noodles, four packs
- Ginger, one slice
- Soy sauce, one tablespoon
- Oil, one tablespoon
- Cilantro, as required

Instructions:
1. Take a large bowl.
2. Add all the ingredients into the bowl.

3. Make the egg mixture.
4. Take a large pan.
5. Heat a pan and then add the oil into the pan.
6. Add the egg mixture on top when the oil heats up.
7. Let the eggs cook from the bottom.
8. Now slowly start to flip the egg.
9. Dish out the egg when both the sides turn golden brown.
10. Garnish the eggs by adding chopped cilantro on top.
11. Your dish is ready to be served.

2.4 Japanese Ramen with Soft Boiled Eggs Recipe

Preparation Time: 30 minutes

Cooking Time: 10 minutes

Serving: 4

Ingredients:

- Chopped chives, one teaspoon
- Butter, two tablespoon
- Salt, to taste
- Black pepper, to taste
- Tamari paste, two teaspoon
- Eggs, four

- Mirin paste, one tablespoon
- Chopped garlic, one teaspoon
- Ramen noodles, four packs

Instructions:
1. Boil the eggs.
2. Make sure to boil the eggs for five minutes only.
3. Take a large pan.
4. Add the butter and let it meltdown.
5. Add in the tamari paste.
6. Mix all the ingredients well.
7. Add the chopped garlic.
8. Add in the rest of the ingredients in the end.
9. Scramble the mixture.
10. Add in the salt and pepper.
11. Boil the ramen noodles according to the instructions on the pack.
12. Drain the noodles and add them into the pan.
13. Mix all the ingredients well and then dish them out.
14. Peel the eggs and place it on the ramen.
15. Garnish the fresh chopped chives on top.
16. Your dish is ready to be served.

2.5 Japanese Miso Ramen with Boiled Eggs Recipe

Preparation Time: 30 minutes

Cooking Time: 10 minutes

Serving: 4

Ingredients:

- Chopped chives, one teaspoon
- Butter, two tablespoon
- Salt, to taste
- Black pepper, to taste
- Miso paste, two teaspoon
- Eggs, four
- Mirin paste, one tablespoon
- Chopped garlic, one teaspoon
- Ramen noodles, four packs

Instructions:
1. Boil the eggs.
2. Make sure to boil the eggs for ten minutes only.

3. Take a large pan.
4. Add the butter and let it meltdown.
5. Add in the miso paste.
6. Mix all the ingredients well.
7. Add the chopped garlic.
8. Add in the rest of the ingredients in the end.
9. Scramble the mixture.
10. Add in the salt and pepper.
11. Boil the ramen noodles according to the instructions on the pack.
12. Drain the noodles and add them into the pan.
13. Mix all the ingredients well and then dish them out.
14. Peel the eggs and place them on the ramen.
15. Garnish the fresh chopped chives on top.
16. Your dish is ready to be served.

2.6 Japanese Bacon, Egg and Cheese Breakfast Ramen Recipe

Preparation Time: 30 minutes

Cooking Time: 10 minutes

Serving: 4

Ingredients:

- Chopped chives, one teaspoon
- Butter, two tablespoon
- Chopped bacon, half pound
- Salt, to taste
- Black pepper, to taste
- Cheese, one cup
- Eggs, four
- Mirin paste, one tablespoon
- Chopped garlic, one teaspoon
- Ramen noodles, four packs

Instructions:
1. Take a large pan.
2. Add the butter and let it meltdown.
3. Add in the chopped bacons.
4. Mix all the ingredients well.
5. Add the chopped garlic.
6. Add in the rest of the ingredients in the end.
7. Scramble the mixture.
8. Add in the salt and pepper.
9. Boil the ramen noodles according to the instructions on the pack.

10. Drain the noodles and add them into the pan.
11. Mix all the ingredients well and then dish them out.
12. Your dish is ready to be served.

2.7 Japanese Ramen with Tofu and Eggs Recipe

Preparation Time: 30 minutes
Cooking Time: 10 minutes
Serving: 4

Ingredients:

- Chopped chives, one teaspoon
- Butter, two tablespoon
- Tofu cubes, half pound
- Salt, to taste
- Black pepper, to taste
- Tamari paste, as required
- Eggs, four
- Mirin paste, one tablespoon
- Chopped garlic, one teaspoon

Instructions:

1. Take a large pan.
2. Add the butter and let it meltdown.
3. Add in the eggs.
4. Add in the tamari paste.
5. Mix the tamari paste and eggs and then add the chopped garlic.
6. Scramble the mixture.
7. Add in the salt and pepper.
8. Add in the tofu cubes and rest of the ingredients in the end.
9. When the eggs are done, dish them out.
10. Add the fresh chopped chives on top.
11. Your dish is ready to be served.

2.8 Japanese Chicken Ramen with Bok Choy and Soy Eggs Recipe

Preparation Time: 30 minutes
Cooking Time: 10 minutes
Serving: 4

Ingredients:

- Onions, half cup
- Rice wine, one tablespoon
- Eggs, four
- Black pepper, to taste
- Salt, to taste
- Cooked chicken, one cup
- Ramen noodles, four packs
- Ginger, one teaspoon
- Bok choy, one cup
- Soy sauce, half cup
- Oil, one tablespoon
- Cilantro, as required

Instructions:

1. Take a large bowl.
2. Add all the ingredients into the bowl.
3. Make the egg mixture.
4. Take a large pan.
5. Heat a pan and then add the oil into the pan.
6. Add the egg mixture on top when the oil heats up.
7. Let the eggs cook from the bottom.
8. Scramble the eggs for ten minutes.
9. Garnish the eggs by adding chopped cilantro on top.
10. Your dish is ready to be served.

2.9 Japanese Egg Tonkotsu Ramen Recipe

Preparation Time: 30 minutes
Cooking Time: 10 minutes
Serving: 4

Ingredients:

- Chopped chives, one teaspoon
- Butter, two tablespoon
- Tonkatsu broth, one cup
- Salt, to taste
- Black pepper, to taste

- Tamari paste, two teaspoon
- Eggs, four
- Mirin paste, one tablespoon
- Chopped garlic, one teaspoon
- Ramen noodles, four packs

Instructions:

1. Take a large pan.
2. Add the butter and let it meltdown.
3. Add in the eggs.
4. Add in the tamari paste.
5. Mix the tamari paste and eggs.
6. Add the chopped garlic.
7. Scramble the mixture.
8. Add in the salt and pepper.
9. Add in the tonkatsu broth and rest of the ingredients in the end.
10. Mix all the ingredients well and then dish them out.
11. Garnish the fresh chopped chives on top.
12. Your dish is ready to be served.

2.10 Japanese Scallops and Egg Ramen Recipe

Preparation Time: 30 minutes

Cooking Time: 10 minutes

Serving: 4

Ingredients:

- Chopped cilantro, one teaspoon
- Butter, two tablespoon
- Chopped scallions, two cups
- Salt, to taste
- Black pepper, to taste
- Tamari paste, two teaspoon
- Eggs, four
- Mirin paste, one tablespoon
- Chopped garlic, one teaspoon
- Ramen noodles, four packs

Instructions:
1. Take a large pan.
2. Add the butter and let it meltdown.
3. Add in the chopped scallions.
4. Add in the tamari paste.
5. Mix all the ingredients well.
6. Add the chopped garlic.
7. Add in the rest of the ingredients in the end.
8. Scramble the mixture.

9. Add in the salt and pepper.
10. Boil the ramen noodles according to the instructions on the pack.
11. Drain the noodles and add them into the pan.
12. Mix all the ingredients well and then dish them out.
13. Garnish the fresh chopped cilantro on top.
14. Your dish is ready to be served.

Chapter 3: The World of Ramen Lunch Recipes

Japanese ramen lunch recipes are full of flavors. There are many varieties of ramen noodles that can be eaten during the lunch time. Following are some easy to make recipes that you can cook today:

3.1 Japanese Ramen Noodle Soup Recipe

Preparation Time: 20 minutes

Cooking Time: 20 minutes

Serving: 4

Ingredients:

- Ramen noodles, two packs
- Miso paste, one teaspoon
- Onion, one cup
- Bell peppers, one cup
- Japanese fresh herbs, half teaspoon
- Water, one cup
- Minced garlic, two tablespoon
- Minced ginger, two tablespoon
- Cilantro, half cup
- Diced carrots, one cup

- Olive oil, two tablespoon
- Water, half cup
- Vegetable stock, two cups
- Chopped tomatoes, one cup

Instructions:
1. Take a pan.
2. Add in the oil and onions.
3. Cook the onions until they become soft and fragrant.
4. Add in the chopped garlic and ginger.
5. Cook the mixture and add the tomatoes into it.
6. Add the spices.
7. Add the miso paste into it when the tomatoes are done.
8. Mix the ingredients carefully and cover the pan.
9. Add the vegetables and rest of the ingredients except the noodles.
10. Let the mixture boil.
11. Add the ramen noodles into the soup mixture.
12. Let the soup cook for ten to fifteen minutes straight.
13. Add cilantro on top.
14. Your dish is ready to be served.

3.2 Japanese Duck Ramen Recipes

Preparation Time: 30 minutes

Cooking Time: 10 minutes

Serving: 4

Ingredients:

- Tomato paste, one cup
- Sliced green onions, half cup
- Mirin paste, one teaspoon
- Cilantro, one cup
- Fresh ginger, one teaspoon
- Miso paste, one tablespoon
- Cooked and shredded duck meat, one cup
- Soy sauce, one tablespoon
- Japanese fresh herbs, half teaspoon
- Fresh shiso leaves, two tablespoon
- Fresh cilantro leaves, half cup
- Chopped tomatoes, half cup
- Ramen, as required

Instructions:

1. Add all the ingredients of the sauce i.e. miso paste, soy sauce, mirin paste and Japanese fresh herbs into a large pan.

2. Add the shredded duck meat, tomato paste, chopped tomatoes and the rest of the ingredients into the mixture.
3. Cook the dish for ten minutes.
4. Add the ramen into the mixture once the sauce is ready.
5. Mix the ramen well.
6. Cook the dish for five minutes.
7. Add the cilantro and the green onions into the dish.
8. Your dish is ready to be served.

3.3 Japanese Sapporo Ramen Recipe

Preparation Time: 30 minutes

Cooking Time: 10 minutes

Serving: 4

Ingredients:

- Bean sprouts, one cup
- Sliced green onions, half cup
- Mirin paste, one teaspoon
- Cilantro, one cup
- Bamboo shoots, one teaspoon
- Miso paste, one tablespoon
- Chashu pork meat, one cup

- Soy sauce, one tablespoon
- Cooking oil, two tablespoon
- Chopped garlic, one teaspoon
- Japanese fresh herbs, half teaspoon
- Fresh shiso leaves, two tablespoon
- Fresh cilantro leaves, half cup
- Dried chili flakes, two teaspoon
- Soft boiled eggs, four
- Ramen, as required

Instructions:
1. Take a large pan.
2. Add the cooking oil and chopped garlic into the pan.
3. Add Chashu pork meat into the pan.
4. Add all the spices into the mixture.
5. Cook the ingredients for five minutes.
6. Add the bean sprouts and ramen into the mixture.
7. Cook all the ingredients well.
8. Peel the soft boiled eggs and add them into the mixture.
9. Cook for five minutes.
10. Garnish the dish with cilantro and green onions.
11. Your dish is ready to be served.

3.4 Japanese Miso Ramen Recipe

Preparation Time: 20 minutes
Cooking Time: 10 minutes
Serving: 4

Ingredients:

- Miso paste, half cup
- Sliced green onions, half cup
- Mirin paste, one teaspoon
- Cilantro, one cup
- Fresh ginger, one teaspoon
- Soy sauce, one tablespoon
- Japanese fresh herbs, half teaspoon
- Fresh shiso leaves, two tablespoon
- Fresh cilantro leaves, half cup
- Minced lemon grass, one teaspoon
- Ramen, as required

Instructions:
1. Heat a large pan.
2. Add the miso paste and the rest of the ingredients into the mixture.
3. Cook the ingredients for ten minutes.

4. Add the ramen into the mixture once the sauce is ready.
5. Mix the ramen well.
6. Cook the dish for five minutes.
7. Add the cilantro into the dish.
8. Your dish is ready to be served.

3.5 Japanese Shoyu Ramen Recipe

Preparation Time: 20 minutes
Cooking Time: 20 minutes
Serving: 4

Ingredients:

- Ramen noodles, two packs
- Spicy chili bean sauce, two teaspoon
- Onion, one cup
- Dashi stock, two cups
- Japanese fresh herbs, half teaspoon
- Water, one cup
- Minced garlic, two tablespoon
- Minced ginger, two tablespoon
- Cilantro, half cup
- Fish cakes, one cup
- Chili oil, two tablespoon

- Shredded nori sheets, half cup
- Sheragi negi, two cups
- Chopped tomatoes, one cup

Instructions:
1. Take a pan.
2. Add in the oil and onions.
3. Cook the onions until they become soft and fragrant.
4. Add in the chopped garlic and ginger.
5. Cook the mixture for a few seconds.
6. Add the spices.
7. Add the sheragi negi into it when the spices are done.
8. Mix the ingredients carefully and cover the pan.
9. Add the fish cakes and rest of the ingredients except the noodles.
10. Let the mixture boil.
11. Add the ramen noodles into the soup mixture.
12. Let the soup cook for ten to fifteen minutes straight.
13. Add shredded nori sheets on top.
14. Your dish is ready to be served.

3.6 Japanese Tantanmen Ramen Recipe

Preparation Time: 30 minutes

Cooking Time: 10 minutes

Serving: 4

Ingredients:

- Minced pork, one cup
- Sliced green onions, half cup
- Tahini paste, one teaspoon
- Cilantro, one cup
- Fresh ginger, one teaspoon
- Oyster sauce, one tablespoon
- Rice wine, three tablespoon
- Soy sauce, one tablespoon
- Japanese fresh herbs, half teaspoon
- Chili oil, two tablespoon
- Fresh cilantro leaves, half cup
- Chopped tomatoes, half cup
- Ramen, as required
- Sesame seeds, half cup
- Bean sprouts, one cup
- Bok choy, one cup

Instructions:

1. Add all the ingredients of the sauce i.e. oyster sauce, soy sauce, rice wine and Japanese fresh herbs into a large pan.
2. Add the vegetables, minced pork, chopped tomatoes and the rest of the ingredients into the mixture.
3. Cook the dish for ten minutes.
4. Add the ramen into the mixture once the sauce is ready.
5. Mix the ramen well.
6. Cook the dish for five minutes.
7. Add the cilantro and the green onions into the dish.
8. Your dish is ready to be served.

3.7 Japanese Spicy Pork Ramen Recipe

Preparation Time: 30 minutes

Cooking Time: 10 minutes

Serving: 4

Ingredients:

- Chili paste, two tablespoon
- Sliced green onions, half cup
- Mirin paste, one teaspoon

- Fresh ginger, one teaspoon
- Miso paste, one tablespoon
- Cooked and shredded pork meat, one cup
- Soy sauce, one tablespoon
- Japanese fresh herbs, half teaspoon
- Fresh shiso leaves, two tablespoon
- Fresh cilantro leaves, half cup
- Chopped tomatoes, half cup
- Ramen, as required

Instructions:
1. Add all the ingredients of the sauce i.e. miso paste, soy sauce, mirin paste and Japanese fresh herbs into a large pan.
2. Add the shredded pork meat, chili paste, chopped tomatoes and the rest of the ingredients into the mixture.
3. Cook the dish for ten minutes.
4. Add the ramen into the mixture once the sauce is ready.
5. Mix the ramen well.
6. Cook the dish for five minutes.
7. Add the green onions into the dish.
8. Your dish is ready to be served.

3.8 Japanese Roast Pork Ramen Recipe

Preparation Time: 30 minutes
Cooking Time: 10 minutes
Serving: 4

Ingredients:

- Shredded nori sheets, two tablespoon
- Sliced green onions, half cup
- Mirin paste, one teaspoon
- Miso paste, one tablespoon
- Roasted and shredded pork meat, one cup
- Soy sauce, one tablespoon
- Japanese fresh herbs, half teaspoon
- Fresh shiso leaves, two tablespoon
- Fresh cilantro leaves, half cup
- Ramen, as required

Instructions:
1. Add all the ingredients of the sauce i.e. miso paste, soy sauce, mirin paste and Japanese fresh herbs into a large pan.
2. Add the roasted pork meat, shiso leaves, chopped tomatoes and the rest of the ingredients into the mixture.

3. Cook the dish for ten minutes.
4. Add the ramen into the mixture once the sauce is ready.
5. Mix the ramen well.
6. Cook the dish for five minutes.
7. Add the shredded nori sheets into the dish.
8. Your dish is ready to be served.

3.9 Japanese Chargrilled Chicken Ramen Recipe

Preparation Time: 30 minutes

Cooking Time: 20 minutes

Serving: 4

Ingredients:

- Chicken stock, two cups
- Crushed garlic, two
- Chicken pieces, one pound
- Salt, to taste
- Black pepper, to taste
- Olive oil, two tablespoon
- Dried white wine, one cup
- Onion, one cup
- All-purpose flour, three tablespoon
- Worcestershire sauce, two

tablespoon
- Softened butter, three tablespoon
- Bay leaf, one
- Fresh thyme, two tablespoon
- Grated or sliced cheese, one cup
- Chopped cilantro, one cup
- Ramen noodles, four packs

Instructions:
1. Take a large skillet.
2. Add the oil and onions into the skillet.
3. Cook the onions until they turn golden brown.
4. Add the crushed garlic into the skillet.
5. Add the spices into the mixture.
6. Add all-purpose flour, Worcestershire sauce and dried white wine.
7. Add the butter and then add the chicken stock and ramen noodles.
8. Grill the chicken pieces over a grill pan.
9. Cut the chicken into long pieces.
10. Add the chicken into the ramen mixture.
11. The dish is ready to be served.

3.10 Japanese Lemongrass, Chicken and Ginger Ramen Recipe

Preparation Time: 30 minutes
Cooking Time: 10 minutes
Serving: 4

Ingredients:

- Tomato paste, one cup
- Sliced green onions, half cup
- Mirin paste, one teaspoon
- Cilantro, one cup
- Dried lemongrass, two teaspoon
- Fresh ginger slices, half cup
- Miso paste, one tablespoon
- Cooked and shredded chicken meat, one cup
- Soy sauce, one tablespoon
- Japanese fresh herbs, half teaspoon
- Fresh shiso leaves, two tablespoon
- Lemon juice, half cup
- Fresh cilantro leaves, half cup
- Chopped tomatoes, half cup
- Ramen, as required

Instructions:

1. Add all the ingredients of the sauce i.e. miso paste, soy sauce, mirin paste and Japanese fresh herbs into a large pan.
2. Add the shredded chicken meat, lemongrass, ginger slices, tomato paste, chopped tomatoes and the rest of the ingredients into the mixture.
3. Cook the dish for ten minutes.
4. Add the ramen into the mixture once the sauce is ready.
5. Mix the ramen well.
6. Cook the dish for five minutes.
7. Add the cilantro and the green onions into the dish.
8. Your dish is ready to be served.

3.11 Japanese Spicy Beef Ramen Recipe

Preparation Time: 30 minutes

Cooking Time: 10 minutes

Serving: 4

Ingredients:

- Chili paste, two tablespoon
- Sliced green onions, half cup
- Mirin paste, one teaspoon

- Fresh ginger, one teaspoon
- Miso paste, one tablespoon
- Cooked and shredded beef meat, one cup
- Soy sauce, one tablespoon
- Chopped garlic, one teaspoon
- Japanese fresh herbs, half teaspoon
- Fresh shiso leaves, two tablespoon
- Fresh cilantro leaves, half cup
- Chopped tomatoes, half cup
- Ramen, as required

Instructions:
1. Add all the ingredients of the sauce i.e. miso paste, soy sauce, mirin paste and Japanese fresh herbs into a large pan.
2. Add the shredded beef meat, chili paste, chopped tomatoes and the rest of the ingredients into the mixture.
3. Cook the dish for ten minutes.
4. Add the ramen into the mixture once the sauce is ready.
5. Mix the ramen well.
6. Cook the dish for five minutes.
7. Add the green onions into the dish.
8. Your dish is ready to be served.

3.12 Japanese Prawn Ramen Recipe

Preparation Time: 20 minutes
Cooking Time: 20 minutes
Serving: 4

Ingredients:

- Ramen noodles, two packs
- Miso paste, one teaspoon
- Onion, one cup
- Prawns, one pound
- Bell peppers, one cup
- Japanese fresh herbs, half teaspoon
- Water, one cup
- Minced garlic, two tablespoon
- Minced ginger, two tablespoon
- Cilantro, half cup
- Diced carrots, one cup
- Olive oil, two tablespoon
- Water, half cup
- Vegetable stock, two cups
- Chopped tomatoes, one cup

Instructions:
1. Take a pan.
2. Add in the oil and onions.
3. Cook the onions until they become soft and fragrant.
4. Add in the chopped garlic and ginger.
5. Cook the mixture and add the tomatoes into it.
6. Add the spices.
7. Add the miso paste into it when the tomatoes are done.
8. Mix the ingredients carefully and cover the pan.
9. Add the prawns, vegetables and rest of the ingredients except the noodles.
10. Let the mixture boil.
11. Add the ramen noodles into the soup mixture.
12. Let the soup cook for ten to fifteen minutes straight.
13. Add cilantro on top.
14. Your dish is ready to be served.

3.13 Japanese Ramen Noodle Salad Recipe

Preparation Time: 20 minutes
Cooking Time: 40 minutes
Serving: 2

Ingredients:
- Ginger powder, one tablespoon
- Chicken shredded, two cups
- Garlic powder, two teaspoon
- Maple syrup, half teaspoon
- Sesame oil, one teaspoon
- Soy sauce, one teaspoon
- Sriracha, one tablespoon
- Lime juice, one tablespoon
- Salt, to taste
- Ramen noodles, four packs
- Pepper, to taste

Instructions:
1. Boil the ramen noodles in a large pot full of water.
2. Drain the noodles when they are cooked.
3. Take a large bowl and add boiled noodles into it.
4. Add the ginger and garlic powder.
5. Mix well so that everything mixes well.

6. Add lime juice, maple syrup, cooked shredded chicken, Japanese red chili and soy sauce.
7. Add the salt and pepper as you like.
8. Add the sesame oil and mix well so that a homogeneous mixture is obtained.
9. Add the sriracha into the mixture.
10. Mix everything well.
11. The salad is ready to be served.

3.14 Japanese Mongolian Beef Ramen Recipe

Preparation Time: 30 minutes
Cooking Time: 10 minutes
Serving: 4

Ingredients:

- Nori paste, two tablespoon
- Sliced green onions, half cup
- Mirin paste, one teaspoon
- Fresh ginger, one teaspoon
- Miso paste, one tablespoon
- Beef meat pieces, one cup
- Soy sauce, one tablespoon
- Mongolian spice, two tablespoon
- Olive oil, two teaspoon

- Chopped garlic, one teaspoon
- Japanese fresh herbs, half teaspoon
- Fresh shiso leaves, two tablespoon
- Fresh cilantro leaves, half cup
- Chopped tomatoes, half cup
- Ramen, as required

Instructions:
1. Add the beef pieces into a pan.
2. Add the Mongolian spice and olive oil into the pan.
3. Cook the beef pieces for ten minutes or until they are completely cooked.
4. Dish out the beef pieces and shred them when cooled.
5. Take a large sauce pan.
6. Add all the ingredients of the sauce into the pan.
7. Add the shredded beef meat, nori paste, chopped tomatoes and the rest of the ingredients into the mixture.
8. Cook the dish for ten minutes.
9. Add the ramen into the mixture once the sauce is ready.
10. Mix the ramen well.
11. Cook the dish for five minutes.
12. Add the green onions into the dish.
13. Your dish is ready to be served.

3.15 Japanese Meatball Ramen Recipe

Preparation Time: 30 minutes
Cooking Time: 20 minutes
Serving: 4

Ingredients:

- Beef stock, two cups
- Crushed garlic, two
- Frozen bacon and beef meatballs, one pound
- Salt, to taste
- Black pepper, to taste
- Olive oil, two tablespoon
- Dried white wine, one cup
- Onion, one cup
- All-purpose flour, three tablespoon
- Worcestershire sauce, two tablespoon
- Softened butter, three tablespoon
- Bay leaf, one
- Fresh thyme, two tablespoon
- Grated or sliced cheese, one cup
- Chopped cilantro, one cup
- Ramen noodles, four packs

Instructions:
1. Take a large skillet.
2. Add the oil and onions into the skillet.
3. Cook the onions until they turn golden brown.
4. Add the crushed garlic into the skillet.
5. Add the spices into the mixture.
6. Add the all-purpose flour, Worcestershire sauce and dried white wine.
7. Add the butter and then add the beef stock and ramen noodles.
8. Fry the frozen meatballs in a pan full of cooking oil.
9. Dish out the meatballs when they turn golden brown on all sides.
10. Add the fried meatballs into the ramen mixture.
11. The dish is ready to be served.

3.16 Japanese Ramen Noodle Skillet with Steak Recipe

Preparation Time: 30 minutes

Cooking Time: 20 minutes

Serving: 4

Ingredients:

- Chicken stock, two cups
- Crushed garlic, two
- Steak meat, one pound
- Salt, to taste
- Black pepper, to taste
- Olive oil, two tablespoon
- Dried white wine, one cup
- Onion, one cup
- All-purpose flour, three tablespoon
- Worcestershire sauce, two tablespoon
- Softened butter, three tablespoon
- Bay leaf, one
- Fresh thyme, two tablespoon
- Grated or sliced cheese, one cup
- Chopped cilantro, one cup
- Ramen noodles, four packs

Instructions:

1. Take a large skillet.
2. Add the oil and onions into the skillet.
3. Cook the onions until they turn golden brown.
4. Add the crushed garlic into the skillet.
5. Add the spices into the mixture.
6. Add all-purpose flour, Worcestershire sauce and dried white wine.
7. Add the butter and then add the chicken stock and ramen noodles.
8. Grill the steak meat over a grill pan.
9. Cut the steak into long pieces.
10. Add the steak pieces on top of the ramen mixture.
11. Garnish the noodles with chopped cilantro.
12. The dish is ready to be served.

3.17 Japanese Cheese Ramen Recipe

Preparation Time: 30 minutes

Cooking Time: 20 minutes

Serving: 4

Ingredients:

- Mushroom sauce, one cup
- Miso paste, one teaspoon
- Onion, one cup

- Ramen noodles, four cups
- Shredded mozzarella cheese, one cup
- Water, one cup
- Bok choy, one cup
- Rice vinegar, one tablespoon
- Minced garlic, two tablespoon
- Minced ginger, two tablespoon
- Cilantro leaves, half cup
- Olive oil, two tablespoon
- Water, half cup
- Vegetable stock, half cup
- Chopped tomatoes, one cup

Instructions:
1. Take a pan.
2. Add in the oil and onions.
3. Cook the onions until they become soft and fragrant.
4. Add in the chopped garlic and ginger.
5. Cook the mixture and add the tomatoes into it.
6. Add the spices.
7. When the tomatoes are done, add the miso paste into it.
8. Mix the ingredients carefully and cover the pan.
9. Add the bok choy and rest of the ingredients.

10. Add the water into the mixture and let the mixture boil.
11. Add the ramen noodles into the mixture.
12. Let the noodles cook for ten to fifteen minutes straight.
13. Add cilantro leaves and shredded cheese on top.
14. Your dish is ready to be served.

3.18 Japanese Ramen Burger Recipe

Preparation Time: 20 minutes

Cooking Time: 20 minutes

Serving: 4

Ingredients:

- Ramen buns, as required
- Minced beef meat, one cup
- Bread crumbs, one cup
- Egg, one
- Chopped parsley, half cup
- Fresh chopped cilantro, half cup
- Salt, to taste
- Black pepper, to taste
- Olive oil, for frying
- Yoghurt, half cup

- Lemon juice, a quarter cup
- Fresh chopped cilantro, two tablespoon
- Butter, one tablespoon

Instructions:
1. Take a large bowl.
2. Add the beef meat, salt, pepper, bread crumbs and egg into it.
3. Mix all the ingredients well.
4. Add the chopped cilantro and parsley into the mixture.
5. Mix the ingredients until they become smooth.
6. Shape the mixture into patties.
7. Add the olive oil in a large pan and cook the patties.
8. Cook the patties until they turn golden brown from both sides.
9. In the meanwhile, in a small bowl, add the yoghurt, lemon juice and fresh cilantro.
10. Mix it to form a paste.
11. Add butter on the ramen and heat them.
12. Add the beef patty on the ramen.
13. Add the paste on top of the patty and cover it with the ramen bun.
14. The ramen burger is ready to be served.

3.19 Japanese Garlic and Shrimp Ramen Recipe

Preparation Time: 20 minutes
Cooking Time: 20 minutes
Serving: 4

Ingredients:

- Ramen noodles, two packs
- Miso paste, one teaspoon
- Onion, one cup
- Shrimps, one pound
- Bell peppers, one cup
- Japanese fresh herbs, half teaspoon
- Water, one cup
- Minced garlic, two tablespoon
- Minced ginger, two tablespoon
- Cilantro, half cup
- Diced carrots, one cup
- Olive oil, two tablespoon
- Water, half cup
- Vegetable stock, two cups
- Chopped tomatoes, one cup

Instructions:

1. Take a pan.
2. Add in the oil and onions.
3. Cook the onions until they become soft and fragrant.
4. Add in the chopped garlic and ginger.
5. Cook the mixture and add the tomatoes into it.
6. Add the spices.
7. Add the miso paste into it when the tomatoes are done.
8. Mix the ingredients carefully and cover the pan.
9. Add the shrimps, vegetables and rest of the ingredients except the noodles.
10. Let the mixture boil.
11. Add the ramen noodles into the soup mixture.
12. Let the soup cook for ten to fifteen minutes straight.
13. Add cilantro on top.
14. Your dish is ready to be served.

3.20 Japanese Beef and Ramen Stir-Fry Recipe

Preparation Time: 30 minutes
Cooking Time: 10 minutes
Serving: 4

Ingredients:

- Ramen noodles, four packs
- Sesame oil, one tablespoon
- Cilantro, one cup
- Sesame seeds, half cup
- Fresh ginger, one teaspoon
- Dark soy sauce, one tablespoon
- Mirin paste, one tablespoon
- Dried shisho leaves, half teaspoon
- Chili garlic sauce, two tablespoon
- Thyme, one tablespoon
- Lemon zest, one teaspoon
- Lemon juice, half cup
- Beef pieces, one pound
- Fresh chopped garlic, half cup
- Fresh basil leaves, a quarter cup
- Vegetable broth, one cup

Instructions:
1. Boil the ramen noodles.
2. Add all the ingredients of the sauce into a wok.
3. Cook the ingredients.
4. Add the beef pieces, lemon juice, thyme, lemon zest and rest of the ingredients into the mixture.

5. Add the ramen noodles into the mixture once the mixture is ready.
6. Mix the ramen noodles well and cook it for five minutes.
7. Add the cilantro into the dish.
8. Your dish is ready to be served.

Chapter 4: The World of Ramen Dinner Recipes

Ramen dinner recipes are well- known all over the world for its mesmerizing flavors and varieties. Following are some amazing and healthy Ramen dinner recipes that you would love to make at home:

4.1 Japanese Parmesan and Garlic Ramen Recipe

Preparation Time: 20 minutes
Cooking Time: 20 minutes
Serving: 4

Ingredients:

- Parmesan cheese, one cup
- Ramen noodles, two packs
- Miso paste, one teaspoon
- Onion, one cup
- Bell peppers, one cup
- Japanese fresh herbs, half teaspoon
- Water, one cup
- Minced garlic, two tablespoon
- Cilantro, half cup
- Diced carrots, one cup

- Olive oil, two tablespoon
- Water, half cup
- Vegetable stock, two cups
- Chopped tomatoes, one cup

Instructions:
1. Take a pan.
2. Add in the oil and onions.
3. Cook the onions until they become soft and fragrant.
4. Add in the chopped garlic.
5. Cook the mixture and add the tomatoes into it.
6. Add the spices.
7. Add the miso paste into it when the tomatoes are done.
8. Mix the ingredients carefully and cover the pan.
9. Add the vegetables and rest of the ingredients except the noodles and parmesan cheese.
10. Let the mixture boil.
11. Add the ramen noodles into the soup mixture.
12. Let the soup cook for ten to fifteen minutes straight.
13. Add cilantro and parmesan cheese on top.
14. Your dish is ready to be served.

4.2 Japanese Ginger and Beef Stir-Fry Ramen Recipe

Preparation Time: 30 minutes
Cooking Time: 10 minutes
Serving: 4

Ingredients:

- Ramen noodles, four packs
- Sesame oil, one tablespoon
- Cilantro, one cup
- Sesame seeds, half cup
- Fresh ginger, two tablespoon
- Dark soy sauce, one tablespoon
- Mirin paste, one tablespoon
- Dried shisho leaves, half teaspoon
- Chili garlic sauce, two tablespoon
- Thyme, one tablespoon
- Lemon zest, one teaspoon
- Lemon juice, half cup
- Beef pieces, one pound
- Fresh basil leaves, a quarter cup
- Vegetable broth, one cup

Instructions:

1. Boil the ramen noodles.
2. Add all the ingredients of the sauce into a wok.
3. Cook the ingredients.
4. Add the beef pieces, chopped ginger, lemon juice, thyme, lemon zest and rest of the ingredients into the mixture.
5. Add the ramen noodles into the mixture once the mixture is ready.
6. Mix the ramen noodles well and cook it for five minutes.
7. Add the cilantro into the dish.
8. Your dish is ready to be served.

4.3 Japanese Peanut and Chicken Ramen Recipe

Preparation Time: 30 minutes
Cooking Time: 20 minutes
Serving: 4

Ingredients:

- Mushroom sauce, one cup
- Miso paste, one teaspoon
- Onion, one cup
- Ramen noodles, four cups
- Peanuts, one cup

- Water, one cup
- Chicken pieces, one cup
- Rice vinegar, one tablespoon
- Minced garlic, two tablespoon
- Minced ginger, two tablespoon
- Cilantro leaves, half cup
- Olive oil, two tablespoon
- Water, half cup
- Chicken stock, half cup
- Chopped tomatoes, one cup

Instructions:
1. Take a pan.
2. Add in the oil and onions.
3. Cook the onions until they become soft and fragrant.
4. Add in the chopped garlic and ginger.
5. Cook the mixture and add the tomatoes into it.
6. Add the spices.
7. When the tomatoes are done, add the chicken stock, and miso paste into it.
8. Mix the ingredients carefully and cover the pan.
9. Add the chicken and rest of the ingredients.
10. Add the water into the mixture and let the mixture boil.
11. Add the ramen noodles into the mixture.

12. Let the soup cook for ten to fifteen minutes straight.
13. Add cilantro leaves and peanuts on top.
14. Your dish is ready to be served.

4.4 Japanese Roasted Chicken Ramen Recipe

Preparation Time: 30 minutes
Cooking Time: 20 minutes
Serving: 4

Ingredients:

- Chicken stock, two cups
- Crushed garlic, two
- Chicken pieces, one pound
- Salt, to taste
- Black pepper, to taste
- Olive oil, two tablespoon
- Dried white wine, one cup
- Onion, one cup
- All-purpose flour, three tablespoon
- Worcestershire sauce, two tablespoon
- Softened butter, three tablespoon
- Bay leaf, one

- Fresh thyme, two tablespoon
- Grated or sliced cheese, one cup
- Chopped cilantro, one cup
- Ramen noodles, four packs

Instructions:
1. Take a large skillet.
2. Add the oil and onions into the skillet.
3. Cook the onions until they turn golden brown.
4. Add the crushed garlic into the skillet.
5. Add the spices into the mixture.
6. Add the all-purpose flour, Worcestershire sauce and dried white wine.
7. Add the butter and then add the chicken stock and ramen noodles.
8. Roast the chicken pieces in a preheated oven.
9. Cut the chicken into long pieces.
10. Add the chicken into the ramen mixture.
11. The dish is ready to be served.

4.5 Japanese Sirarcha and Shrimp Ramen Recipe

Preparation Time: 20 minutes
Cooking Time: 20 minutes
Serving: 4

Ingredients:

- Ramen noodles, two packs
- Miso paste, one teaspoon
- Onion, one cup
- Shrimps, one pound
- Bell peppers, one cup
- Japanese fresh herbs, half teaspoon
- Water, one cup
- Minced garlic, two tablespoon
- Minced ginger, two tablespoon
- Cilantro, half cup
- Diced carrots, one cup
- Olive oil, two tablespoon
- Sirarcha sauce, half cup
- Fish stock, two cups
- Chopped tomatoes, one cup

Instructions:
1. Take a pan.
2. Add in the oil and onions.
3. Cook the onions until they become soft and fragrant.
4. Add in the chopped garlic and ginger.
5. Cook the mixture and add the tomatoes into it.
6. Add the spices.
7. Add the miso paste and sirarcha into it when the tomatoes are done.
8. Mix the ingredients carefully and cover the pan.
9. Add the shrimps, vegetables and rest of the ingredients except the noodles.
10. Let the mixture boil.
11. Add the ramen noodles into the soup mixture.
12. Let the soup cook for ten to fifteen minutes straight.
13. Add cilantro on top.
14. Your dish is ready to be served.

4.6 Japanese Bacon Ramen Soup Recipe

Preparation Time: 20 minutes
Cooking Time: 20 minutes
Serving: 4

Ingredients:

- Ramen noodles, two packs
- Miso paste, one teaspoon
- Onion, one cup
- Chopped bacon, one cup
- Japanese fresh herbs, half teaspoon
- Water, one cup
- Minced garlic, two tablespoon
- Minced ginger, two tablespoon
- Cilantro, half cup
- Olive oil, two tablespoon
- Water, half cup
- Chicken stock, two cups
- Chopped tomatoes, one cup

Instructions:
1. Take a pan.

2. Add in the oil and onions.
3. Cook the onions until they become soft and fragrant.
4. Add in the chopped garlic and ginger.
5. Cook the mixture and add the tomatoes into it.
6. Add the spices.
7. Add the chopped bacon into it when the tomatoes are done.
8. Mix the ingredients carefully and cover the pan.
9. Add the rest of the ingredients except the noodles.
10. Let the mixture boil.
11. Add the ramen noodles into the soup mixture.
12. Let the soup cook for ten to fifteen minutes straight.
13. Add cilantro on top.
14. Your dish is ready to be served.

4.7 Japanese Sweet and Sour Pork Ramen Recipe

Preparation Time: 30 minutes
Cooking Time: 10 minutes
Serving: 4

Ingredients:

- Sweet and sour sauce, one cup
- Chili paste, two tablespoon
- Sliced green onions, half cup
- Mirin paste, one teaspoon
- Fresh ginger, one teaspoon
- Miso paste, one tablespoon
- Cooked and shredded pork meat, one cup
- Soy sauce, one tablespoon
- Japanese fresh herbs, half teaspoon
- Fresh shiso leaves, two tablespoon
- Fresh cilantro leaves, half cup
- Chopped tomatoes, half cup
- Ramen, as required

Instructions:

1. Add all the ingredients of the sauce i.e. miso paste, soy sauce, mirin paste and Japanese fresh herbs into a large pan.
2. Add the shredded pork meat, sweet and sour sauce, chopped tomatoes and the rest of the ingredients into the mixture.
3. Cook the dish for ten minutes.
4. Add the ramen into the mixture once the sauce is ready.
5. Mix the ramen well.
6. Cook the dish for five minutes.
7. Add the green onions into the dish.
8. Your dish is ready to be served.

4.8 Japanese Cheesy Tuna Ramen Recipe

Preparation Time: 30 minutes

Cooking Time: 20 minutes

Serving: 4

Ingredients:

- Miso paste, one teaspoon
- Onion, one cup
- Ramen noodles, four cups
- Shredded mozzarella cheese, one cup
- Water, one cup
- Tuna pieces, one cup

- Rice vinegar, one tablespoon
- Minced garlic, two tablespoon
- Minced ginger, two tablespoon
- Cilantro leaves, half cup
- Olive oil, two tablespoon
- Water, half cup
- Fish stock, half cup
- Chopped tomatoes, one cup

Instructions:
1. Take a pan.
2. Add in the oil and onions.
3. Cook the onions until they become soft and fragrant.
4. Add in the chopped garlic and ginger.
5. Cook the mixture and add the tomatoes into it.
6. Add the spices.
7. When the tomatoes are done, add the miso paste into it.
8. Mix the ingredients carefully and cover the pan.
9. Add the tuna pieces and rest of the ingredients.
10. Add the water into the mixture and let the mixture boil.
11. Add the ramen noodles into the mixture.
12. Let the noodles cook for ten to fifteen minutes straight.

13. Add cilantro leaves and shredded cheese on top.
14. Your dish is ready to be served.

4.9 Japanese Ramen and Tomato Soup Recipe

Preparation Time: 30 minutes
Cooking Time: 10 minutes
Serving: 4

Ingredients:

- Tomato paste, one cup
- Sliced green onions, half cup
- Mirin paste, one teaspoon
- Cilantro, one cup
- Fresh ginger, one teaspoon
- Miso paste, one tablespoon
- Soy sauce, one tablespoon
- Japanese fresh herbs, half teaspoon
- Fresh shiso leaves, two tablespoon
- Fresh cilantro leaves, half cup
- Chopped tomatoes, half cup
- Ramen, as required

Instructions:

1. Add all the ingredients of the sauce i.e. miso paste, soy sauce, mirin paste and Japanese fresh herbs into a large pan.
2. Add the tomato paste, chopped tomatoes and the rest of the ingredients into the mixture.
3. Cook the dish for ten minutes.
4. Add the ramen into the mixture once the sauce is ready.
5. Mix the ramen well.
6. Cook the dish for five minutes.
7. Add the cilantro and the green onions into the dish.
8. Your dish is ready to be served.

4.10 Japanese Chili Ramen Recipe

Preparation Time: 20 minutes
Cooking Time: 20 minutes
Serving: 4

Ingredients:

- Ramen noodles, two packs
- Miso paste, one teaspoon
- Onion, one cup
- Chili paste, one tablespoon
- Japanese fresh herbs, half teaspoon

- Water, one cup
- Minced garlic, two tablespoon
- Cilantro, half cup
- Chopped green chilies, one cup
- Olive oil, two tablespoon
- Vegetable stock, two cups
- Chopped tomatoes, one cup

Instructions:
1. Take a pan.
2. Add in the oil and onions.
3. Cook the onions until they become soft and fragrant.
4. Add in the chopped garlic.
5. Cook the mixture and add the tomatoes into it.
6. Add the spices.
7. Add the chili paste into it when the tomatoes are done.
8. Mix the ingredients carefully and cover the pan.
9. Add the chopped green chilies and rest of the ingredients except the noodles.
10. Let the mixture boil.
11. Add the ramen noodles into the mixture.
12. Let the ingredients cook for ten to fifteen minutes straight.
13. Add cilantro on top.
14. Your dish is ready to be served.

4.11 Japanese Chicken and Mushroom Ramen Recipe

Preparation Time: 20 minutes
Cooking Time: 20 minutes
Serving: 4

Ingredients:

- Ramen noodles, two packs
- Miso paste, one teaspoon
- Onion, one cup
- Chicken pieces, one cup
- Japanese fresh herbs, half teaspoon
- Water, one cup
- Minced garlic, two tablespoon
- Cilantro, half cup
- Sliced mushrooms, one cup
- Olive oil, two tablespoon
- Water, half cup
- Chicken stock, two cups
- Chopped tomatoes, one cup

Instructions:

1. Take a pan.
2. Add in the oil and onions.
3. Cook the onions until they become soft and fragrant.
4. Add in the chopped garlic.
5. Cook the mixture and add the tomatoes into it.
6. Add the spices.
7. Add the chicken pieces into it when the tomatoes are done.
8. Mix the ingredients carefully and cover the pan.
9. Add the mushrooms and rest of the ingredients except the noodles.
10. Let the mixture boil.
11. Add the ramen noodles into the soup mixture.
12. Let the soup cook for ten to fifteen minutes straight.
13. Add cilantro on top.
14. Your dish is ready to be served.

4.12 Japanese Parmesan Chicken Ramen Recipe

Preparation Time: 20 minutes

Cooking Time: 20 minutes

Serving: 4

Ingredients:

- Parmesan cheese, one cup
- Ramen noodles, two packs
- Miso paste, one teaspoon
- Onion, one cup
- Chicken pieces, one cup
- Japanese fresh herbs, half teaspoon
- Water, one cup
- Minced garlic, two tablespoon
- Cilantro, half cup
- Olive oil, two tablespoon
- Water, half cup
- Chicken stock, two cups
- Chopped tomatoes, one cup

Instructions:
1. Take a pan.
2. Add in the oil and onions.
3. Cook the onions until they become soft and fragrant.
4. Add in the chopped garlic.
5. Cook the mixture and add the tomatoes into it.
6. Add the spices.
7. Add the miso paste into it when the tomatoes are done.

8. Add the chicken pieces and rest of the ingredients except the noodles and parmesan cheese.
9. Let the mixture boil.
10. Add the ramen noodles into the soup mixture.
11. Let the soup cook for ten to fifteen minutes straight.
12. Add cilantro and parmesan cheese on top.
13. Your dish is ready to be served.

4.13 Japanese Chicken Lo Mein Ramen Recipe

Preparation Time: 30 minutes

Cooking Time: 10 minutes

Serving: 4

Ingredients:

- Diced cabbage, one cup
- Brown sugar, two tablespoon
- Sliced green onions, half cup
- Mirin paste, one teaspoon
- Fresh ginger, one teaspoon
- Miso paste, one tablespoon
- Cooked and shredded chicken meat, one cup

- Soy sauce, one tablespoon
- Shiitake mushrooms, one cup
- Japanese fresh herbs, half teaspoon
- Fresh shiso leaves, two tablespoon
- Fresh cilantro leaves, half cup
- Chopped tomatoes, half cup
- Ramen, as required

Instructions:

1. Add all the ingredients of the sauce i.e. miso paste, soy sauce, mirin paste and Japanese fresh herbs into a large pan.
2. Add the shredded chicken, diced cabbage, brown sugar, shitake mushrooms and the rest of the ingredients into the mixture.
3. Cook the dish for ten minutes.
4. Add the ramen into the mixture once the sauce is ready.
5. Mix the ramen well.
6. Cook the dish for five minutes.
7. Add the green onions into the dish.
8. Your dish is ready to be served.

4.14 Japanese Shrimp Ramen Recipe

Preparation Time: 30 minutes
Cooking Time: 10 minutes

Serving: 4

Ingredients:

- Shiitake mushrooms, one cup
- Diced carrots, one cup
- Sliced green onions, half cup
- Mirin paste, one teaspoon
- Fresh ginger, one teaspoon
- Miso paste, one tablespoon
- Devilled shrimps, one cup
- Soy sauce, one tablespoon
- Chopped garlic, one teaspoon
- Japanese fresh herbs, half teaspoon
- Fresh shiso leaves, two tablespoon
- Fresh cilantro leaves, half cup
- Chopped tomatoes, half cup
- Ramen, as required

Instructions:
1. Add all the ingredients of the sauce i.e. miso paste, soy sauce, mirin paste and Japanese fresh herbs into a large pan.

2. Add the devilled shrimps, carrots, mushrooms, chopped tomatoes and the rest of the ingredients into the mixture.
3. Cook the dish for ten minutes.
4. Add the ramen into the mixture once the sauce is ready.
5. Mix the ramen well.
6. Cook the dish for five minutes.
7. Add the green onions into the dish.
8. Your dish is ready to be served.

4.15 Japanese Green Pepper and Chicken Ramen Recipe

Preparation Time: 20 minutes
Cooking Time: 20 minutes
Serving: 4

Ingredients:

- Ramen noodles, two packs
- Miso paste, one teaspoon
- Onion, one cup
- Chicken pieces, one cup
- Japanese fresh herbs, half teaspoon
- Water, one cup
- Minced garlic, two tablespoon

- Cilantro, half cup
- Green pepper, one cup
- Olive oil, two tablespoon
- Water, half cup
- Chicken stock, two cups
- Chopped tomatoes, one cup

Instructions:
1. Take a pan.
2. Add in the oil and onions.
3. Cook the onions until they become soft and fragrant.
4. Add in the chopped garlic.
5. Cook the mixture and add the tomatoes into it.
6. Add the spices.
7. Add the chicken pieces into it when the tomatoes are done.
8. Mix the ingredients carefully and cover the pan.
9. Add the green pepper and rest of the ingredients except the noodles.
10. Let the mixture boil.
11. Add the ramen noodles into the soup mixture.
12. Let the soup cook for ten to fifteen minutes straight.
13. Add cilantro on top.
14. Your dish is ready to be served.

4.16 Japanese Creamy Tonkotsu Ramen Recipe

Preparation time: 30 minutes
Cooking Time: 10 minutes
Serving: 4

Ingredients:

- Heavy cream, one cup
- Sliced green onions, half cup
- Mirin paste, one teaspoon
- Cilantro, one cup
- Fresh ginger, one teaspoon
- Miso paste, one tablespoon
- Soy sauce, one tablespoon
- Japanese fresh herbs, half teaspoon
- Chopped leeks, two tablespoon
- Chicken meat, one cup
- Tonkatsu broth, one cup
- Fresh cilantro leaves, half cup
- Minced lemon grass, one teaspoon
- Ramen, as required

Instructions:

1. Add all the ingredients of the sauce i.e. miso paste, soy sauce, mirin paste and Japanese fresh herbs into a large pan.
2. Add the heavy cream and the rest of the ingredients into the mixture.
3. Cook the dish for ten minutes.
4. Add the ramen into the mixture once the sauce is ready.
5. Mix the ramen well.
6. Close the lid of the instant pot.
7. Cook the dish for five more minutes.
8. Add the cilantro into the dish.
9. Your dish is ready to be served.

4.17 Japanese Miso and Crispy Pork Ramen Recipe

Preparation Time: 20 minutes
Cooking Time: 10 minutes
Serving: 4

Ingredients:

- Miso paste, half cup
- Sliced green onions, half cup
- Mirin paste, one teaspoon
- Cilantro, one cup

- Fresh ginger, one teaspoon
- Soy sauce, one tablespoon
- Japanese fresh herbs, half teaspoon
- Fresh shiso leaves, two tablespoon
- Fresh cilantro leaves, half cup
- Minced lemon grass, one teaspoon
- Ramen, as required
- Pork strips, one cup
- Corn starch, two teaspoon
- Cooking oil, as required

Instructions:
1. Heat a large pan.
2. Add the cooking oil and let it heat.
3. Mix the pork and cornstarch and add it into the heated oil.
4. Cook the pork well for about five minutes.
5. Dish out the pork strips and set aside when done.
6. Add the miso paste and the rest of the ingredients into the mixture.
7. Cook the ingredients for ten minutes.
8. Add the ramen into the mixture once the sauce is ready.
9. Mix the ramen well.
10. Cook the dish for five minutes.
11. Add the crispy pork on top.

12. Add the cilantro into the dish.
13. Your dish is ready to be served.

4.18 Japanese Shio and Pork Ramen Recipe

Preparation Time: 20 minutes
Cooking Time: 20 minutes
Serving: 4

Ingredients:

- Ramen noodles, two packs
- Cooked and shredded pork, one cup
- Spicy chili bean sauce, two teaspoon
- Onion, one cup
- Dashi stock, two cups
- Japanese fresh herbs, half teaspoon
- Water, one cup
- Minced garlic, two tablespoon
- Minced ginger, two tablespoon
- Cilantro, half cup
- Chili oil, two tablespoon
- Shredded nori sheets, half cup
- Sheragi negi, two cups
- Chopped tomatoes, one cup

Instructions:

1. Take a pan.
2. Add in the oil and onions.
3. Cook the onions until they become soft and fragrant.
4. Add in the chopped garlic and ginger.
5. Cook the mixture for a few seconds.
6. Add the spices.
7. Add the sgeragi negi and shredded pork into it when the spices are done.
8. Mix the ingredients carefully and cover the pan.
9. Let the mixture boil.
10. Add the ramen noodles into the soup mixture.
11. Let the soup cook for ten to fifteen minutes straight.
12. Add shredded nori sheets on top.
13. Your dish is ready to be served.

4.19 Japanese Ramen Noodle Coleslaw Recipe

Preparation Time: 20 minutes
Cooking Time: 40 minutes
Serving: 2

Ingredients:

- Coleslaw mix, two cups
- Maple syrup, half teaspoon
- Sesame oil, one teaspoon
- Soy sauce, one teaspoon
- Salt, to taste
- Ramen noodles, four packs
- Pepper, to taste

Instructions:
1. Boil the ramen noodles in a large pot full of water.
2. Drain the noodles when they are cooked.
3. Take a large bowl and add boiled noodles into it.
4. Add the rest of the ingredients into the bowl.
5. Add the salt and pepper as you like.
6. Add the sesame oil and mix well so that a consistent mixture is obtained.
7. The salad is ready to be served.

4.20 Japanese Instant Ramen Noodle Recipe

Preparation Time: 10 minutes
Cooking Time: 10 minutes
Serving: 4

Ingredients:

- Water, two cups
- Ramen noodles, two pack
- Mirin paste, one tablespoon
- Mix spice, half cup
- Dashi powder, two tablespoon
- Fresh shiso leaves, a quarter cup
- Sesame oil, one tablespoon

Instructions:
1. Take a large pan.
2. Add all the ingredients into the pan.
3. Cook the ingredients for ten minutes.
4. Garnish it with shiso leaves.
5. Your dish is ready to be served.

Chapter 5: The World of Vegetarian Ramen Recipes

Ramen noodles are a comfort food for everyone in the world. It tends to be straightforward and economical, and you can make it extravagant and jam-loaded with beautiful and healthy vegetables and flavors. You should try all of these twenty yummy vegetarian recipes at home as they are easy to make and will surely make your day:

5.1 Japanese Spicy Vegetarian Ramen Recipe

Preparation Time: 30 minutes
Cooking Time: 10 minutes
Serving: 4

Ingredients:

- Chili paste, two tablespoon
- Sliced green onions, half cup
- Mirin paste, one teaspoon
- Fresh ginger, one teaspoon
- Miso paste, one tablespoon
- Chopped carrots, one cup
- Soy sauce, one tablespoon
- Shredded zucchini, one cup
- Blanched peas, one cup

- Chopped garlic, one teaspoon
- Japanese fresh herbs, half teaspoon
- Fresh shiso leaves, two tablespoon
- Fresh cilantro leaves, half cup
- Chopped tomatoes, half cup
- Ramen, as required

Instructions:

1. Add all the ingredients of the sauce i.e. miso paste, soy sauce, mirin paste and Japanese fresh herbs into a large pan.
2. Add the vegetables, chili paste, chopped tomatoes and the rest of the ingredients into the mixture.
3. Cook the dish for ten minutes.
4. Add the ramen into the mixture once the sauce is ready.
5. Mix the ramen well.
6. Cook the dish for five minutes.
7. Add the green onions into the dish.
8. Your dish is ready to be served.

5.2 Japanese Shiitake Mushroom Ramen Recipe

Preparation Time: 30 minutes
Cooking Time: 10 minutes
Serving: 4

Ingredients:

- Bean sprouts, one cup
- Sliced green onions, half cup
- Mirin paste, one teaspoon
- Cilantro, one cup
- Bamboo shoots, one teaspoon
- Miso paste, one tablespoon
- Shiitake mushrooms, one cup
- Soy sauce, one tablespoon
- Cooking oil, two tablespoon
- Chopped garlic, one teaspoon
- Japanese fresh herbs, half teaspoon
- Fresh shiso leaves, two tablespoon
- Fresh cilantro leaves, half cup
- Dried chili flakes, two teaspoon
- Soft boiled eggs, four
- Ramen, as required

Instructions:
1. Take a large pan.
2. Add the cooking oil and chopped garlic into the pan.
3. Add the shiitake mushrooms into the pan.

4. Add all the spices into the mixture.
5. Cook the ingredients for five minutes.
6. Add the bean sprouts and ramen into the mixture.
7. Cook all the ingredients well.
8. Peel the soft boiled eggs and add them into the mixture.
9. Cook for five minutes.
10. Garnish the dish with cilantro and green onions.
11. Your dish is ready to be served.

5.3 Japanese Miso Vegetarian Ramen Noodle Soup Recipe

Preparation Time: 20 minutes

Cooking Time: 20 minutes

Serving: 4

Ingredients:

- Ramen noodles, two packs
- Miso paste, one teaspoon
- Onion, one cup
- Bean sprouts, one cup
- Japanese fresh herbs, half teaspoon
- Water, one cup

- Minced garlic, two tablespoon
- Minced ginger, two tablespoon
- Cilantro, half cup
- Diced carrots, one cup
- Olive oil, two tablespoon
- Blanched peas, half cup
- Vegetable stock, two cups
- Chopped tomatoes, one cup

Instructions:
1. Take a pan.
2. Add in the oil and onions.
3. Cook the onions until they become soft and fragrant.
4. Add in the chopped garlic and ginger.
5. Cook the mixture and add the tomatoes into it.
6. Add the spices.
7. Add the miso paste into it when the tomatoes are done.
8. Mix the ingredients carefully and cover the pan.
9. Add the carrot, peas, bean sprouts and rest of the ingredients except the noodles.
10. Let the mixture boil.
11. Add the ramen noodles into the soup mixture.
12. Let the soup cook for ten to fifteen minutes straight.

13. Add cilantro on top.
14. Your dish is ready to be served.

5.4 Japanese Teriyaki Tofu Ramen Recipe

Preparation Time: 30 minutes
Cooking Time: 10 minutes
Serving: 4

Ingredients:

- Teriyaki sauce, one cup
- Sliced green onions, half cup
- Mirin paste, one teaspoon
- Cilantro, one cup
- Bamboo shoots, one teaspoon
- Miso paste, one tablespoon
- Soy sauce, one tablespoon
- Cooking oil, two tablespoon
- Chopped garlic, one teaspoon
- Japanese fresh herbs, half teaspoon
- Fresh shiso leaves, two tablespoon
- Fresh cilantro leaves, half cup
- Dried chili flakes, two teaspoon
- Tofu cubes, one cup

- Ramen, as required

Instructions:
1. Take a large pan.
2. Add the cooking oil and chopped garlic into the pan.
3. Add the tofu cubes into the pan.
4. Add all the spices into the mixture.
5. Cook the ingredients for five minutes.
6. Add the teriyaki sauce and ramen into the mixture.
7. Cook all the ingredients well.
8. Cover the pan for five minutes.
9. Garnish the dish with cilantro and green onions.
10. Your dish is ready to be served.

5.5 Japanese Tonkotsu Vegetarian Ramen Recipe

Preparation Time: 30 minutes
Cooking Time: 10 minutes
Serving: 4

Ingredients:

- Chopped chives, one teaspoon

- Butter, two tablespoon
- Tonkotsu broth, one cup
- Salt, to taste
- Black pepper, to taste
- Tamari paste, two teaspoon
- Mix vegetables, two cups
- Mirin paste, one tablespoon
- Chopped garlic, one teaspoon
- Ramen noodles, four packs

Instructions:
1. Take a large pan.
2. Add the butter and let it meltdown.
3. Add in the tamari paste.
4. Mix the tamari paste for two minutes.
5. Add the chopped garlic and mixed vegetables.
6. Add in the salt and pepper.
7. Add in the tonkotsu broth and rest of the ingredients in the end.
8. Mix all the ingredients well and then dish them out.
9. Garnish the fresh chopped chives on top.
10. Your dish is ready to be served.

5.6 Japanese Pantry Vegetarian Ramen Recipe

Preparation Time: 10 minutes
Cooking Time: 10 minutes
Serving: 4

Ingredients:

- Garlic powder, one teaspoon
- Soy sauce, a quarter cup
- Sliced green onions, half cup
- Ginger powder, one teaspoon
- Lemon juice, half cup
- Miso paste, one tablespoon
- Sirarcha sauce, two tablespoon
- Vegetables (of your choice), one cup
- Japanese fresh herbs, half teaspoon
- Ketchup, two tablespoon
- Fresh cilantro leaves, half cup
- Sliced scallions, half cup
- Ramen, as required
- Sesame oil, two tablespoon

Instructions:

1. Take a large saucepan.
2. Add the sesame oil and scallions into the pan.
3. Cook the scallions for a few minutes.
4. Add the garlic powder.
5. Add the ketchup and sirarcha into the mixture.
6. Cook the ingredients for two minutes.
7. Add the vegetables of your choice into the pan.
8. Cook the ingredients well.
9. Add the rest of the ingredients along with the ramen noodles.
10. Cook the mixture for ten minutes.
11. Garnish the ramen with green onions and cilantro on top.
12. Your dish is ready to be served.

5.7 Japanese Marinated Tofu and Vegetable Ramen Recipe

Preparation Time: 30 minutes
Cooking Time: 20 minutes
Serving: 4

Ingredients:

- Vegetable stock, two cups
- Crushed garlic, two
- Tofu cubes, one pound

- Salt, to taste
- Black pepper, to taste
- Olive oil, two tablespoon
- Dried white wine, one cup
- Onion, one cup
- All-purpose flour, three tablespoon
- Worcestershire sauce, two tablespoon
- Softened butter, three tablespoon
- Bay leaf, one
- Fresh thyme, two tablespoon
- Soy sauce, one cup
- Chopped cilantro, one cup
- Ramen noodles, four packs

Instructions:

1. Marinate the tofu cubes in soy sauce for ten to fifteen minutes.
2. Take a large skillet.
3. Add the oil and onions into the skillet.
4. Cook the onions until they turn golden brown.
5. Add the crushed garlic into the skillet.
6. Add the spices into the mixture.
7. Add all-purpose flour, Worcestershire sauce and dried white wine.
8. Add the butter and then add the vegetable stock and ramen noodles.

9. Add the tofu cubes into the ramen mixture.
10. Cook the mixture for ten minutes.
11. The dish is ready to be served.

5.8 Japanese Creamy Vegan Ramen Recipe

Preparation Time: 30 minutes
Cooking Time: 10 minutes
Serving: 4

Ingredients:

- Heavy cream, one cup
- Sliced green onions, half cup
- Mirin paste, one teaspoon
- Cilantro, one cup
- Fresh ginger, one teaspoon
- Miso paste, one tablespoon
- Soy sauce, one tablespoon
- Japanese fresh herbs, half teaspoon
- Chopped leeks, two tablespoon
- Tonkatsu broth, one cup
- Fresh cilantro leaves, half cup
- Minced lemon grass, one teaspoon
- Ramen, as required

Instructions:

1. Add all the ingredients of the sauce i.e. miso paste, soy sauce, mirin paste and Japanese fresh herbs into a large pan.
2. Add the heavy cream and the rest of the ingredients into the mixture.
3. Cook the dish for ten minutes.
4. Add the ramen into the mixture once the sauce is ready.
5. Mix the ramen well.
6. Close the lid of the instant pot.
7. Cook the dish for five more minutes.
8. Add the cilantro into the dish.
9. Your dish is ready to be served.

5.9 Japanese Creamy Sesame Ramen Broth Recipe

Preparation Time: 20 minutes
Cooking Time: 20 minutes
Serving: 4

Ingredients:

- Ramen noodles, two packs
- Miso paste, one teaspoon

- Onion, one cup
- Sesame seeds, one cup
- Japanese fresh herbs, half teaspoon
- Water, one cup
- Minced garlic, two tablespoon
- Minced ginger, two tablespoon
- Cilantro, half cup
- Heavy cream, one cup
- Olive oil, two tablespoon
- Water, half cup
- Vegetable stock, two cups
- Chopped tomatoes, one cup

Instructions:
1. Take a pan.
2. Add in the oil and onions.
3. Cook the onions until they become soft and fragrant.
4. Add in the chopped garlic and ginger.
5. Cook the mixture and add the tomatoes into it.
6. Add the spices.
7. Add the miso paste into it when the tomatoes are done.
8. Mix the ingredients carefully and cover the pan.
9. Add the sesame seeds and the rest of the ingredients except the noodles.

10. Let the mixture boil.
11. Add the ramen noodles and heavy cream into the broth mixture.
12. Let the broth cook for ten to fifteen minutes straight.
13. Add cilantro on top.
14. Your dish is ready to be served.

5.10 Japanese Spicy Broccoli Ramen Recipe

Preparation Time: 30 minutes
Cooking Time: 10 minutes
Serving: 4

Ingredients:

- Chili paste, two tablespoon
- Sliced green onions, half cup
- Mirin paste, one teaspoon
- Fresh ginger, one teaspoon
- Miso paste, one tablespoon
- Chopped broccoli, one cup
- Soy sauce, one tablespoon
- Chopped garlic, one teaspoon
- Japanese fresh herbs, half teaspoon
- Fresh shiso leaves, two tablespoon

- Fresh cilantro leaves, half cup
- Chopped tomatoes, half cup
- Ramen, as required

Instructions:

1. Add all the ingredients of the sauce i.e. miso paste, soy sauce, mirin paste and Japanese fresh herbs into a large pan.
2. Add the broccoli, chili paste, chopped tomatoes and the rest of the ingredients into the mixture.
3. Cook the dish for ten minutes.
4. Add the ramen into the mixture once the sauce is ready.
5. Mix the ramen well.
6. Cook the dish for five minutes.
7. Add the green onions into the dish.
8. Your dish is ready to be served.

5.11 Japanese Cauliflower Ramen Recipe

Preparation Time: 20 minutes
Cooking Time: 10 minutes
Serving: 4

Ingredients:

- Miso paste, half cup
- Sliced green onions, half cup
- Cauliflower florets, two cups
- Cilantro, one cup
- Fresh ginger, one teaspoon
- Soy sauce, one tablespoon
- Japanese fresh herbs, half teaspoon
- Fresh shiso leaves, two tablespoon
- Fresh cilantro leaves, half cup
- Minced lemon grass, one teaspoon
- Ramen, as required

Instructions:
1. Heat a large pan.
2. Add the cauliflower florets and the rest of the ingredients into the mixture.
3. Cook the ingredients for ten minutes.
4. Add the ramen into the mixture once the sauce is ready.
5. Mix the ramen well.
6. Cook the dish for five minutes.
7. Add the cilantro into the dish.
8. Your dish is ready to be served.

5.12 Japanese Hot and Sour Dashi Ramen Recipe

Preparation Time: 30 minutes

Cooking Time: 10 minutes

Serving: 4

Ingredients:

- Hot and sour sauce, one cup
- Sliced green onions, half cup
- Mirin paste, one teaspoon
- Fresh ginger, one teaspoon
- Miso paste, one tablespoon
- Dashi stock, one cup
- Soy sauce, one tablespoon
- Japanese fresh herbs, half teaspoon
- Fresh shiso leaves, two tablespoon
- Fresh cilantro leaves, half cup
- Chopped tomatoes, half cup
- Ramen, as required

Instructions:

1. Add all the ingredients of the sauce i.e. miso paste, soy sauce, mirin paste and Japanese fresh herbs into a large pan.

2. Add the dashi stock, hot and sour sauce, chopped tomatoes and the rest of the ingredients into the mixture.
3. Cook the dish for ten minutes.
4. Add the ramen into the mixture once the sauce is ready.
5. Mix the ramen well.
6. Cook the dish for five minutes.
7. Add the green onions into the dish.
8. Your dish is ready to be served.

5.13 Japanese Spicy Carrot Ramen Recipe

Preparation Time: 30 minutes
Cooking Time: 10 minutes
Serving: 4

Ingredients:

- Chili paste, two tablespoon
- Sliced green onions, half cup
- Mirin paste, one teaspoon
- Fresh ginger, one teaspoon
- Miso paste, one tablespoon
- Chopped carrots, one cup
- Soy sauce, one tablespoon
- Chopped garlic, one teaspoon

- Japanese fresh herbs, half teaspoon
- Fresh shiso leaves, two tablespoon
- Fresh cilantro leaves, half cup
- Chopped tomatoes, half cup
- Ramen, as required

Instructions:
1. Add all the ingredients of the sauce i.e. miso paste, soy sauce, mirin paste and Japanese fresh herbs into a large pan.
2. Add the carrots, chili paste, chopped tomatoes and the rest of the ingredients into the mixture.
3. Cook the dish for ten minutes.
4. Add the ramen into the mixture once the sauce is ready.
5. Mix the ramen well.
6. Cook the dish for five minutes.
7. Add the green onions into the dish.
8. Your dish is ready to be served.

5.14 Japanese Vegan Shōyu Ramen with Potatoes Recipe

Preparation Time: 20 minutes

Cooking Time: 20 minutes

Serving: 4

Ingredients:

- Ramen noodles, two packs
- Chopped potatoes, one cup
- Spicy chili bean sauce, two teaspoon
- Onion, one cup
- Dashi stock, two cups
- Japanese fresh herbs, half teaspoon
- Minced garlic, two tablespoon
- Minced ginger, two tablespoon
- Cilantro, half cup
- Chili oil, two tablespoon
- Shredded nori sheets, half cup
- Sheragi negi, two cups
- Chopped tomatoes, one cup

Instructions:
1. Take a pan.
2. Add in the oil and onions.
3. Cook the onions until they become soft and fragrant.
4. Add in the chopped garlic and ginger.
5. Cook the mixture for a few seconds.
6. Add the spices.
7. Add the sgeragi negi and chopped potatoes into it when the spices are done.
8. Mix the ingredients carefully and cover the pan.
9. Add the rest of the ingredients except the noodles.

10. Let the mixture boil.
11. Add the ramen noodles into the mixture.
12. Add shredded nori sheets on top.
13. Your dish is ready to be served.

5.15 Japanese Ginger Ramen Recipe

Preparation Time: 10 minutes

Cooking Time: 10 minutes

Serving: 4

Ingredients:

- Water, two cups
- Ramen noodles, two pack
- Ginger paste, one tablespoon
- Mix spice, half cup
- Dashi powder, two tablespoon
- Fresh shiso leaves, a quarter cup
- Sesame oil, one tablespoon

Instructions:
1. Take a large pan.
2. Add all the ingredients into the pan.
3. Cook the ingredients for ten minutes.
4. Garnish it with shiso leaves.
5. Your dish is ready to be served.

5.16 Japanese Vegan Ramen Taco Recipe

Preparation Time: 10 minutes

Cooking Time: 10 minutes

Serving: 4

Ingredients:

- Water, two cups
- Ramen noodle plates, two pack
- Mixed vegetables, one cup
- Ginger paste, one tablespoon
- Mix spice, half cup
- Dashi powder, two tablespoon
- Fresh shiso leaves, a quarter cup
- Sesame oil, one tablespoon

Instructions:
1. Take a large pan.
2. Add the vegetables and rest of the filling ingredients into the pan.
3. Cook the ingredients for ten minutes.
4. Switch off the stove.
5. Boil the ramen noodle plates in boiling water for one minute each.
6. Turn them into taco shape.
7. Add the prepared filling mixture into the taco.

8. Garnish the tacos with shiso leaves.
9. Your dish is ready to be served.

5.17 Japanese Vegetarian Spicy Peanut Tempeh Ramen Recipe

Preparation Time: 30 minutes
Cooking Time: 10 minutes
Serving: 4

Ingredients:

- Peanut sauce, one cup
- Sliced green onions, half cup
- Chili paste, one teaspoon
- Mirin paste, one teaspoon
- Cilantro, one cup
- Bamboo shoots, one teaspoon
- Miso paste, one tablespoon
- Soy sauce, one tablespoon
- Cooking oil, two tablespoon
- Chopped garlic, one teaspoon
- Japanese fresh herbs, half teaspoon
- Fresh shiso leaves, two tablespoon
- Fresh cilantro leaves, half cup
- Dried chili flakes, two teaspoon

- Tempeh cubes, one cup
- Ramen, as required

Instructions:
1. Take a large pan.
2. Add the cooking oil and chopped garlic into the pan.
3. Add the tempeh cubes into the pan.
4. Add all the spices into the mixture.
5. Cook the ingredients for five minutes.
6. Add the peanut sauce and ramen into the mixture.
7. Cook all the ingredients well.
8. Cover the pan for five minutes.
9. Garnish the dish with cilantro and green onions.
10. Your dish is ready to be served.

5.18 Japanese Spicy Soy Milk Ramen Recipe

Preparation Time: 30 minutes
Cooking Time: 10 minutes
Serving: 4

Ingredients:

- Soy milk, one cup

- Chili paste, one tablespoon
- Sliced green onions, half cup
- Mirin paste, one teaspoon
- Cilantro, one cup
- Fresh ginger, one teaspoon
- Miso paste, one tablespoon
- Soy sauce, one tablespoon
- Japanese fresh herbs, half teaspoon
- Fresh shiso leaves, two tablespoon
- Fresh cilantro leaves, half cup
- Minced lemon grass, one teaspoon
- Ramen, as required

Instructions:

1. Add all the ingredients of the sauce i.e. miso paste, soy sauce, mirin paste and Japanese fresh herbs into a large pan.
2. Add the soy milk and the rest of the ingredients into the mixture.
3. Cook the dish for ten minutes.
4. Add the ramen into the mixture once the sauce is ready.
5. Mix the ramen well.
6. Cook the dish for five minutes.
7. Add the cilantro into the dish.
8. Your dish is ready to be served.

5.19 Japanese Vegetarian Ginger and Scallion Ramen Recipe

Preparation Time: 10 minutes
Cooking Time: 10 minutes
Serving: 4

Ingredients:

- Water, two cups
- Ramen noodles, two pack
- Ginger slices, half cup
- Mix vegetables, one cup
- Chopped scallions, half cup
- Mix spice, half cup
- Dashi powder, two tablespoon
- Fresh shiso leaves, a quarter cup
- Sesame oil, one tablespoon

Instructions:
1. Take a large pan.
2. Add all the vegetables and oil into the pan.
3. Add the spices and sauces into the pan.
4. Cook the ingredients for five minutes and add the ramen noodles.
5. Cook the ingredients for ten minutes.

6. Garnish it with ginger slices and scallions on top.
7. Your dish is ready to be served.

5.20 Japanese Crispy Sesame Tofu Ramen Recipe

Preparation Time: 20 minutes
Cooking Time: 10 minutes
Serving: 4

Ingredients:

- Sesame seeds, half cup
- Sliced green onions, half cup
- Mirin paste, one teaspoon
- Cilantro, one cup
- Fresh ginger, one teaspoon
- Soy sauce, one tablespoon
- Japanese fresh herbs, half teaspoon
- Fresh shiso leaves, two tablespoon
- Fresh cilantro leaves, half cup
- Minced lemon grass, one teaspoon
- Ramen, as required
- Tofu cubes, one cup
- Corn starch, two teaspoon
- Cooking oil, as required

Instructions:
1. Heat a large pan.
2. Add the cooking oil and let it heat.
3. Mix the tofu cubes, sesame seeds and cornstarch in a bowl.
4. Add the tofu cubes into the heated oil.
5. Cook the tofu well for about five minutes.
6. Dish out the tofu cubes and set aside when done.
7. Add the miso paste and the rest of the ingredients into the mixture.
8. Cook the ingredients for ten minutes.
9. Add the ramen into the mixture once the sauce is ready.
10. Mix the ramen well.
11. Cook the dish for five minutes.
12. Add the crispy sesame tofu on top.
13. Add the cilantro into the dish.
14. Your dish is ready to be served.

Conclusion

Japanese noodle soups aka ramen is one of the easiest comfort food that you can prepare at home. Ramen soups come in different varieties. You can have vegetarian soups as well as non-vegetarian soups. All these soups are healthy and full of taste for ramen lovers around the world.

After reading this book, you will realize that making your favorite Japanese food at home is not difficult at all. In this book, we discussed in detail the history and origin of ramen. The various ingredients used in cooking ramen have also been mentioned in this book. This cookbook includes 70 recipes that contain breakfast, lunch, dinner, and vegetarian recipes. You can easily make these recipes at home without supervision of any kind. So, start cooking today and enjoy cooking your delicious ramen at home.

Printed in Great Britain
by Amazon